Walking Each Other Home

Walking Each Other Home

Reflections about Living a Christian Life
from an Older Dad to His Daughter

Peter C. Wilcox

RESOURCE *Publications* · Eugene, Oregon

WALKING EACH OTHER HOME
Reflections about Living a Christian Life from an Older Dad to His Daughter

Resource Publications
An Imprint of Wipf and Stock Publishers
199 W. 8th Ave., Suite 3
Eugene, OR 97401

www.wipfandstock.com

PAPERBACK ISBN: 978-1-5326-1806-2
HARDCOVER ISBN: 978-1-4982-4329-2
EBOOK ISBN: 978-1-4982-4328-5

Manufactured in the U.S.A.   MAY 4, 2017

To my daughter, Colleen, whose constant love, energy and happy disposition has kept me young through the years. May your life always reflect your goodness.

Contents

Introduction

DEAR COLLEEN:

It is with great love that I write these thoughts to you. My hope is that long after I am gone, these reflections about life might be a source of strength, inspiration and comfort to you. Through the years, as you continue to grow, you will face many challenges and perhaps these thoughts will be my way of staying connected to you.

You are a young adult now and doing very well. Having already finished your Master's degree, you have a very good job at Shepherd Pratt Hospital which you seem to find challenging and fulfilling. More recently, we have talked about your desire to possibly pursue a Ph.D. or PsyD. degree to further your education. With time, I'm sure you will decide about this. It could be a way of providing other job opportunities for you in the future.

I am older now, 75 to be precise, but I have been thinking about and writing parts of this book for the last eight years. I hope with the years comes some wisdom that I would like to share with you. I guess being an older Dad has some advantages and disadvantages. If age gives one more experiences, then I hope that my experiences might serve as a way for me to share my life with you. That is where the wisdom comes in and I hope and pray that these reflections will allow me to share with you some of the things I have learned through the years. On the other hand, being an older

Dad might limit the amount of time we have together and so these reflections are a way for me to try and stay connected to you long after I am gone. Ever since you were born almost twenty–seven years ago, my constant prayer has been that the Lord would bless me with good health so that like I have often said to you, "I can get you raised!" So far, He has answered my prayer and I am very grateful.

As you know Colleen, life is full of choices. Sometimes, the choices you make will seem to be extremely important. At other times, they might seem to be insignificant. But you will find that each and every choice you make in your life will influence the kind of person you will become. Your looks don't matter at all. You don't need to be good at sports. You don't need to be popular. You need not be smarter than others. Those things are nice and useful, and pleasing. But they won't by themselves, determine the kind of person you will be. And—they won't make you happy. Looks change. People can sometimes treat us unfairly for no seemingly good reason. Friends come and go as our lives take us in new directions, different jobs, and far away places. Ultimately, you will discover that your happiness will flow from the kind of person you are.

These reflections on life, Colleen, are freely offered to you and you are certainly free to accept or reject them. In fact, as you grow, that is what you will be called upon to do and that is the beauty of you becoming your own person. You are completely unique, loved by God, Mom and me and so many other people. And as you go through the years, the Lord is forming you, shaping you to become your own unique person. These thoughts are simply offered for your reflection as a way of helping in this process. Perhaps some of these reflections will be meaningful to you now, perhaps others, later, maybe some not at all. That's ok. That's the way it needs to be as you make your way on your journey through life. When you read them, please don't feel that you have to agree with all of them and please don't feel guilty if you simply disagree with some of them. That's ok too. I simply offer them to you with my love, for your thought and reflection.

1

On the Importance of Our Faith

As I HAVE GROWN older, Colleen, I have realized that when life is stripped down to its very essentials, it is surprising how simple things become. Fewer and fewer things really matter, and those that do, matter a great deal more. This is what I have come to believe about our faith. I have come to see how important my faith is and how it affects every dimension of my life.

A. Getting It Backwards

When I was growing up, our faith was an important part of our family. We went to church every Sunday, participated in the sacrament of reconciliation, and sometimes attended the parish mission. However, despite all of this, for some reason, I "got it backwards" about God's love. Somehow, for reasons I still don't completely understand, I grew up feeling as though I had to earn God's love. I thought I had to "become good" first, and then God would love me. It felt like I had to earn God's love. Somehow, I grew up not realizing that God loves me unconditionally. That no matter what I do, His love is always there for me.

This is what I have come to call the "principle of creative love." This is the belief that we are "loved first," independent of what we do or accomplish. His love for us actually creates the love within each of us that draws us out of ourselves to love one another.

A deceased Jesuit priest, Pierre Teilhard de Chardin (1881–1955), was both a scientist and mystic. He spent many years ministering to the people of China. Chardin used to ask why so many sincere, good people did not believe in God. His answer was sympathetic, not judgmental. He felt that they must not have heard about God in the correct way. His religious writings are an attempt to make faith in God more palatable for those who, for whatever reason, are struggling with it.

Many people struggle with their understanding of who God is and the role He plays in their life. Maybe the most important thing to remember in life, Colleen, is God's unconditional love for you. Believing this can shape your entire life. The challenge is to truly believe it. In a sense, we know it intellectually because we have been taught this from our earliest days. Sometimes, we "sort of" believe it but to believe it in a way that applies to each of us can have a huge impact on your life.

In a sense, it's almost too good to be true. It's so different from the way we "humans" usually love others. Even though we try not to, many of us put "conditions" on the way we love others. Some of these conditions might sound something like this. "I will love others who love me." "I will love others if I like them." "I will love others who are nice to me." "I will love others who agree with me." "I will love those whom I like to be around and do things with." There are so many conditions that sometimes we are not even aware of them.

And this is why God's "unconditional" love is sometimes difficult to understand and accept. His way of loving is so different from ours and our own experience. As I grew up thinking, sometimes we can think that God will only love us after "we become good" or only if we don't sin. But His love for us has none of these conditions and this is why it is so different from the way we love and why it is almost too good to be true.

Colleen, God loves us even though we are sinners. There are no conditions attached to God's love for us. The Gospels are full of stories where Jesus loves people first and with no conditions and you can see in these stories how his love changes people's lives.

And that is why, if we can believe this, then it will change our lives too. If we can accept His unconditional love for us, then we will want to respond to this kind of love with the way we try to love and the way we try to live our lives. Then we will go and try to always become better in response to—and in gratitude for—His unconditional love for us. This is why His love for us can have a huge impact on the way we live our lives.

My hope is that you will always remember this Colleen—not simply in an intellectual way but in a way that "seeps down into your bones," so that it becomes a motivating factor in the way that you live each day of your life.

B. Putting the Pieces Together

Some years ago, Bill told me a story about his childhood. When he was a young boy, he said that his parents kept a giant jigsaw puzzle set up on a table in their living room. His father, who had started this tradition, always hid the box top. The idea was to put the pieces together without knowing the picture ahead of time. Different members of the family and visiting friends would work on it, sometimes for only a few minutes at a time, until after several weeks hundreds and hundreds of pieces would each find their place.

Bill said that over the years, his family finished dozens of these puzzles. In the end, he became quite good at it and took a certain satisfaction in being the first one to see where a piece went or how two groups of pieces fit together. He especially loved the time when the first hint of a pattern would emerge and he could see what had been there, hidden, all along.

The puzzle table had been his father's birthday present to his mother. He could still see him setting up the table and pouring the pieces of that first puzzle from the box onto the tabletop. Bill was only three or four then and he didn't really understand his mother's delight. They hadn't explained the game to him, thinking that he was too young to participate. But he wanted to participate, even then.

Alone in the living room early one morning, he climbed on a chair and spread out the hundreds of loose pieces lying on the table. The pieces were fairly small; some were brightly colored and some dark and shadowy. The dark ones seemed like spiders or bugs. They were ugly and a little frightening. They made him feel uncomfortable. Gathering up a few of these, he climbed down and hid them under one of the cushions on the sofa. For several weeks, whenever he was alone in the living room, he would climb up on the chair, take a few more dark pieces, and add them to the ones under the cushion.

As you can imagine, this first puzzle took the family a very long time to finish! Frustrated, his mother finally counted the pieces and realized that more than a hundred were missing. She asked Bill if he had seen them. He told her then what he had done with the pieces he didn't like and she rescued them and completed the puzzle. He remembered watching her do this. As piece after dark piece was put in place and the picture emerged, Bill was astounded. It was quite beautiful, a peaceful scene of a deserted beach. Without the pieces he had hidden, the puzzle made no sense.

In some way, Colleen, life is like this jigsaw puzzle. In a sense, we are always trying to put the pieces of our lives together without really knowing the full picture ahead of time. Life provides all the pieces. Some of our pieces are very positive and pleasant—like the happiness of a success or a time of celebration. But other pieces can be difficult and dark—like the pieces Bill wanted to hide under the sofa cushions. These might be sad or painful events but together these make up the pieces of our own life's puzzle.

This is where our faith comes into play, Colleen. It is our Christian faith that gives us a way of putting the pieces of our lives together. It gives us a blueprint, so to speak, to navigate our way through life. It will help sustain you through the "ups and downs" of life. Life is full of good times and difficult times and your faith can be the main factor in helping you cope with the different things that happen to you in life. Turning to God in times of trial and difficulties can help immensely. For example, when our son, and your brother, Andrew, was stillborn at full term thirty-two years ago, I don't know what I would have done if it wasn't for my faith. It didn't make the loss any less traumatic and sorrowful, but it at least gave Mom and me a way to try and understand it. And even that was terribly difficult! It was one of those pieces of our life's puzzle that was extremely painful. And as you go through the years, Colleen, I'm sure there will be difficulties and sorrows and it's your faith that will help you through those difficult times.

C. A Blueprint

There are so many reasons why our faith is so important to us, Colleen, and why Mom and me hope that it is and will continue to be important to you. We know that you don't go to the Catholic Church anymore but our prayer for you in this regard is that one day you will return. Our hope is that you will see your faith as a kind of blueprint that will help you navigate your way through life. It's like a compass that can help guide you through life. It's from our belief in God that we learn how to live according to certain values and moral principles and this helps us in our daily actions and activities. If we had no faith, I suppose we would have to acquire those guidelines somewhere else. However, with our faith we can at least know how we should be acting. Not that we are always able to live up to those beliefs as much as we might like to. Sometimes, we stumble and fall, but that's ok . . . the Lord is always there to pick us up and help us carry on. But I suppose our daily struggle is to live out the meaning and implications of our faith each and every day. Moreover, there will always be people who won't agree with you in terms of your values and principles and this is where it takes courage and conviction on your part to not allow other people to sway you as some might try to do.

D. The God in Our Gut

As Catholics, Colleen, we believe that faith is a gift that is freely given to us but it must also be nurtured throughout our lives because this gift can also be lost. God is always offering us His love and this gift of faith but we have to respond to it. The way you nurture your faith life is to cultivate your relationship with the Lord and there are many ways to do this. What you want to try and do is to develop a personal relationship with God. But how would you do this? Well, how would you develop a friendship? You would want to talk with that person, spend time with them, go places with them, enjoy their company, etc. And it's the same in our relationship with God. It's very important in our spiritual lives to see God as our friend, as our companion on this journey in life and we can do this with each of the three persons of the Trinity.

First of all, Colleen, try to see God as your father just like a Dad. In fact, one of the neatest words describing God in the Old Testament is the word "Abba." This name means seeing God as our Father or "Daddy." It was a very familial term used by the Old Testament people because they believed that God was like a father to them. God was the person who loved them unconditionally and took care of them and would always be there for them. This is who God the Father is for us too. He is not some mean, punishing God who is out to catch us when we do something wrong but rather a loving, caring Father who wants only the best for us.

The way we look at Jesus is also important for our spiritual lives. He is our Lord, our Savior, our Brother, who loved us so much that He was willing to suffer and die for us in order to save us and gain for us the possibility of everlasting life. If we see Jesus as our friend, our buddy so to speak, it will allow us to speak to Him easily and freely like we would do with any other friend. It's seeing Him as a real person that allows us to deepen our relationship with Him. One of the reasons why it's important to read and slowly pray over the New Testament is because this is the way we come to understand today who Jesus really was and what He was truly like. Then, as His followers, we are able to try and imitate His way of thinking and behaving in our own lives.

One spiritual writer sees Jesus as "the mercy of God." In other words, if we want to know who this God is that we believe in—all we have to do is to look at Jesus. This one word, "mercy" is the word that describes God for us. The Lord *is* the mercy of God for us and if we can see Him in this way, then that will encourage us to love Him and draw near to Him.

The third person of the Trinity that we believe in is the Holy Spirit. Some people feel that the Holy Spirit is difficult to understand but really when you think about it we believe that the Spirit dwells within each of us. If you want a "job description" of the Holy Spirit, one that I like is that the job of the Holy Spirit is to create in each of us a clearer image of the Lord. How does He do this? By dwelling in our hearts and inspiring us to constantly do the right thing. The inspired thoughts that we have like "I should do this . . . " or "wouldn't it be good if I did that . . . " are really graces or inspired thoughts that the Holy Spirit gives us to constantly help shape and mold us into that clearer image of Jesus. Another way to look at what the Holy Spirit does for us is to see Him "nudging" us to do the right thing, encouraging us to hang in there when we get discouraged, helping us to have the strength to avoid doing the wrong thing. One of the gifts that I pray to the Holy Spirit for is the gift of wisdom. This is the gift that enables us to be wise, to know what we should say or do in a given situation. You can be smart but not wise, Colleen. Wisdom is the gift that helps us find the right words to say in a difficult situation or to know within ourselves how to act when others around us are acting differently or possibly making fun of us because of our beliefs or way of acting. This gift of wisdom is truly a gift of the Holy Spirit and one for which we should earnestly pray.

2

Wanting to Be Spiritual
but Not Religious

A STRANGE THING IS happening in the Western world today. As the number of people participating in our churches is dramatically decreasing, the number of people interested in spirituality is proportionately increasing. We are witnessing a drastic decline in church life right in the midst of a spiritual renaissance. What is happening?

There seems to be a divorce taking place between spirituality and participating in the life of the church, between those who understand themselves to be on a spiritual quest and those inside our churches. As one person told me: "I am a good Christian, a sincere, God-serving person, but I don't need the church—I can pray just as well at home."

This way of thinking can be true if you are a theist, Colleen, but it can never be true for a Christian. Part of the very essence of Christianity is to be together in a concrete community, with all the real human faults that are there and the tensions that this will bring us. Spirituality, for a Christian, can never be an individualistic quest, the pursuit of God outside of community, family, and church. Jesus tells us that anyone who says that he or she loves an invisible God in heaven and is unwilling to deal with a visible neighbor on earth is a liar since no one can love a God who cannot be seen if he or she cannot love a neighbor who can be seen.

Maybe a couple of examples will help explain what is going on. Sam was a young social worker living in the inner city. He was a Roman Catholic, although he attended church only occasionally, had basically no private prayer in his life, and no longer even tried to live the church's moral teachings regarding sex and marriage. These he openly flaunted and considered a medieval hang-up. He was, however, deeply committed to the church's social teachings, had a passion for justice, and was quite generous in serving the poor.

One day he asked me: "do you really think that God gives a damn whether you say your morning and evening prayers, whether you hold a grudge against someone who has hurt you, or whether you sleep with someone you aren't married to? Do you really believe God cares about these petty little things? As Christians, we are always so hung up on these little private things, that we neglect the big picture—the fact that half the world goes to bed hungry every night and nobody gives a damn. Justice, not our petty little prayer lives, is what is important, religiously and morally. Why are we forever hung up on what's insignificant?"

Similarly, Donna is a woman of faith, faithful in her marriage, a good mother, and scrupulously honest. She reads spiritual books, prays daily on her own, and even leads retreats on spirituality. There are no major inconsistencies in her life regarding private prayer or personal integrity. In addition, she has a deep concern for justice, is committed to various causes, and is involved with several groups who are trying to help the poor; in fact, some of her family and friends consider her a bit of a social justice radical. Moreover, she is also a woman of some warmth and graciousness. She enjoys celebrating life with others, has a good sense of humor, knows what to do with a good bottle of wine, and seemingly has little bitterness or anger about life.

In many ways, Donna is an exemplary Christian person. But she doesn't go to church. In her view of things, personal involvement within a concrete church community is not that important. She is not particularly negative about the church and even attends occasionally. For her, indifference is the bigger issue.

These are just two examples, Colleen, of why people don't go to church anymore. There are certainly many other reasons. Sometimes, these reasons stem from the very visible human side of the church. We all know of scandals; sometimes it's the way people are treated by those in authority in the church; at other times, we see the glaring imperfections in those who have leadership positions in the church and the decisions they make. Sometimes, people disagree with the church's teachings on certain issues and so they stop going. At other times, we see people who go to church regularly but then don't treat those people around them with love and compassion. All of these reasons are simply the "human" side of the church. They are evident to everyone. To put it simply—the church has many weaknesses—and sometimes these are very glaring.

However, it is also important to understand, Colleen, that research on the question of declining church attendance shows that most people who do not go to church anymore do not have theological questions about the nature of the church. Nor are they angry about things going on in the church. This is not to say that these are not important issues for some people. However, research has discovered that, like Donna, indifference and a culture of individualism are the two main reasons for declining church attendance. Most people who are not at church on Sunday are not at home brooding about the church's faults or thinking about some theological question about the church. They are sleeping, shopping, jogging in the park, watching baseball or football games, working on their lawns and gardens, and visiting with family and friends. They do not have huge questions about the church. It's like they are on sabbatical. They are busy doing other things.

It's important to understand that the things people complain about Colleen, are not the real church. The real church is *all of us*—*we* are the church and God has given us the church in order to lead us to heaven. All of us *together* are the church and just like each person has strengths and limitations—so the church, that is made up of human beings, has strengths and limitations. In other words, the church is certainly not perfect because its members are not perfect. However, over the course of the years, you will have to make choices about your faith and your participation in the life of the church. Through the years, we have tried to instill in you a love for our faith as well as a desire to participate in the life of the church. But as you have grown older, you have decided not to go to church anymore. I'm sure you have your reasons for this. This decision has been very painful for us and we continue to pray that one day you will understand the importance of the church and begin to participate again.

On a more positive side, we believe that the Catholic Church is the church that Jesus established and which has continued through the Apostles down through the centuries. And it is in and through our participation in the life of the church that we receive the grace we need to lead holy, Christian lives. Each time we go to church, we participate with others in our community of faith to worship and pray together. Each time we go to church, we hear the Word of God proclaimed and that Word helps guide us to live our lives in a certain way. Each time we go to church and receive the Body and Blood of Jesus in the Eucharist, we receive the graces we need to live our lives as Christians—to make those daily choices that shape the kind of person that we are and that we want to become.

There will always be people who say they don't need the church, that it doesn't help them in any way, that they can still be a good person even if they don't go to church. But this kind of thinking misses the point of what the church is all about. The church is not some building or some people handing down a bunch of rules. The church is us—we are the church and the church is given to us by God for our salvation. It is at Mass that we are given the opportunity to receive the sacraments, to worship and pray together and to grow in holiness.

A. Having "Good Religion"

Jim Haas, an historian, writer, musician, and educator said one time that to think that the universe came to be by chance—that order comes from chaos—is comparable to believing that we could throw all the parts of a Lexus up into the air, and they would land as a fully assembled automobile.

Where does the universe come from? One of the first principles of metaphysics, Colleen, is that something doesn't come from nothing. Can we have design without a "designer?" Could we come upon a Lexus and believe that it just happened, that no one made it? To carry this analogy even further—if someone gave us a Lexus, would we not express our gratitude? Whom then, do we thank for this entire universe?

"Good religion" Colleen, begins with a sense of awe and gratitude. The word "Eucharist," the word for our Mass means "to give thanks." We thank God for the gift of our universe and for all of creation. We thank God, in Jesus, who entered history. We thank the Holy Spirit who lives within us.

"Good religion," then, gathers us as a grateful people to give thanks. And, at its best, organized religion is organized goodness. While it is easy to focus on the failings of people in the church, it's so easy to miss all the good—the schools, the hospitals, the soup kitchens like the Franciscan Center, the worldwide charities, and on and on. The Catholic Church has sponsored these ministries for years—long before there were such organizations like social services. We could list page after page of so many ministries that the church does to help people day to day, person to person. They simply wouldn't exist without the power of the organization of the church.

We don't live in a morally neutral universe. If we are not hearing the voice of God that lifts us up, we can too easily listen to many other voices—the voice of our own egos, the voice of the world that leads to selfishness and self-centeredness.

At the end of each day, Colleen, you might want to ask yourself if you have brought love and peace and caring to where you are living and working. Then the world is a bit more the world of God. And—we need a place where we can thank God for His many blessings. We need a place where we can gather with other believers and feed on His word and presence in order to create a better world. We need a church—where organized religion will continue to be "good religion."

3

On Becoming Your Own Person

In Margery William's little book, entitled *The Velveteen Rabbit*, there is a lovely dialogue between the Skin Horse and the Rabbit. The wise character in the story is the Skin Horse who is trying to help the Rabbit learn how to become real.

"What is Real?" asked the Rabbit one day. "Does it mean having things that buzz inside you and a stick-out handle?"

"Real isn't how you are made," said the Skin Horse. "It's a thing that happens to you. When a child loves you for a long, long time, not just to play with, but REALLY loves you, then you become Real."

"Does it hurt?" asked the Rabbit.

"Sometimes," said the Skin Horse, for he was always truthful. "When you are Real you don't mind being hurt."

"Does it happen all at once, like being wound up," he asked, "or bit by bit?"

"It doesn't happen all at once," said the Skin Horse. "You become. It takes a long time. That's why it doesn't often happen to people who break easily, or have sharp edges, or who have to be carefully kept. Generally, by the time you are Real, most of your hair has been loved off, and your eyes drop out and you get loose in the joints and very shabby. But these things don't matter at all, because once you are Real you can't be ugly, except to people who don't understand."[1]

Maybe one of the most difficult things for all of us, Colleen, is to become Real—to become our own person—the person that God created us to be with all our own uniqueness, beauty, and individual qualities. It's something that we work on every day of our lives in one way or another. Using our gifts and talents, making choices each day are all part of this process to become our own person.

One reason why this can be difficult in our culture is because there are so many forces trying to influence us. Certain segments of our society say: "be this way . . . act that way . . . dress in this way . . . do this . . . don't do that." It's like there are so many voices in our head trying to gain our attention and wanting to influence our decisions. That's why you have to know what is helpful in our culture, Colleen, and what is not, in order to use the good parts and disregard the bad parts. And that is not always easy. Just look at what our culture says to young women about what is important in life—about how one should look, what one should wear, and how one should act. You have to be able to sift out the good from the bad in order to become your own person. Otherwise, you will just be bounced back and forth according to whatever "the culture" is saying and emphasizing.

Sometimes, Colleen, we have to go against the culture in terms of how we think and what we value. These you must choose yourself. And this is where our faith can serve as a kind of blueprint for what is important in life. You can't let anyone or any society determine these for you. And sometimes it is difficult to go against something in our culture or to choose something different from our friends. This takes a lot of courage because sometimes people will try to make you feel bad, odd, or different because of what you believe. But that's ok—because you are being true to yourself and becoming your own person. And eventually what you can do is find other people who think like you do and hold the same values. Then, you can support each other.

1. Williams, *The Velveteen Rabbit*, 5.

In Mitch Albom's book, *Tuesdays with Morrie*, Morrie, who is dying from ALS, talks about the influence that our culture has on us in relation to becoming our own person. "The culture we have does not make people feel good about themselves," he said. "We're teaching the wrong things. And you have to be strong enough to say if the culture doesn't work, don't buy it. Create your own. Most people can't do it."[2] Then, he went on to explain that sometimes we have to build our own little subculture. "I don't mean you disregard every rule of your community. I don't go around naked, for example. I don't run through red lights. The little things, I can obey. But the big things—how we think, what we value—those you must choose yourself. You can't let anyone—or any society—determine those for you."[3]

A. Beauty is on the Inside

In our culture, Colleen, there is such an emphasis today on beauty. That is why there are so many businesses trying to sell you things on how to become more beautiful. For women, there are probably thousands of products that you can buy that claim to do something to your body to help you become more physically attractive. It's the same for men. There is such an emphasis on the body—the way we look physically.

While all of this may be important to some people, it's important to understand that real beauty in a person lies on the *inside*. It's what is inside a person that truly counts. This is what really matters. I suppose in some ways, anyone can do something to the *outside* of the body in order to become more attractive. But the real issue is—how do we become more beautiful on the inside? And what does that really mean?

First of all, I think it means to always strive to be a truly good person. Back in the 1950's, there was a man by the name of Dag Hammarskjold, who was the secretary general of the

---

2. Albom, *Tuesdays with Morrie*, 35–36.
3. Ibid., 155.

United Nations. This was really a very prestigious position and he was truly a remarkable person. He wrote a wonderful little book called *Markings*, and in this book he said: "Goodness is something so simple, always to live for others, never to seek one's own advantage."[4] He thought that to be a truly good person, you had to live not just for yourself but for others. To be a good person meant trying to be more selfless rather than selfish. This was the way he tried to live his life and how he encouraged others.

Secondly, I think that becoming more beautiful on the inside has something to do with having a roadmap within yourself, to know what kind of person you want to become and then trying to follow that map within yourself as best you can each day.

Thirdly, I think it means reflecting on the qualities you want to possess as a woman and striving to live that way each day. I believe those qualities are what we find in living the Christian life. Being a person of integrity, living a virtuous life, trying to become a more loving person, becoming kind, understanding and gentle, treating others with dignity and respect, striving to live justly, trying to help others in whatever ways you can—all of these as well as other qualities that you believe are important—make you beautiful on the inside. What a world we would have if the emphasis in our culture would encourage this kind of beauty. These are so much more important than beauty on the outside.

B. On Discovering Your Values

Maybe one of the most difficult and challenging things to do in life, Colleen, is to discover what values you want to live by. As I have previously mentioned, in our society, there are so many voices trying to get our attention so that they can influence our decisions about life. This is what marketing is really all about, isn't it? On one level, these companies are usually trying to sell us something. But, on a deeper level, they are trying to convince us about what is really important in life. This is why discovering what is truly

4. Hammarskjold, *Markings*, 87.

important to us is so necessary because these values will shape the way we live.

Some people live their lives by what others say. These people are constantly being tossed around like a boat in a turbulent sea. They are at the whim of what other people think and say. For awhile a certain thing is an important value for them; then for awhile something else becomes important. As a result, they go through life without an anchor or any real guidelines and values to live by.

It's important in life, Colleen, to have a core—a center to who you are. In a sense, this gives us a roadmap to follow in life. Sometimes, we might not follow it as well as we would like to—but that's ok. We all take detours so to speak, but we can always go back to the main road and get back on track again. And that's why it's important to know what our main values are in life. These values become the guidelines by which we try to live our lives. And once we have discovered them, it gives us a way of evaluating all the other voices in our society. When our society says something that goes against your core values—your center—you simply dismiss it. For example, when society says that the end all and be all of life is making money, becoming popular or powerful, and you realize that these go against what is important to you, then you have a way of evaluating that idea against one of your core values. Or, when society says that you should dress in a certain way in order to look good but that goes against one of your core values—then you simply dismiss it. Having these kinds of core values at the center of who you are, keeps you from being tossed around by everything that comes "down the pike" which is constantly changing. These values are very important for becoming a certain kind of person who is trying to live your life in a certain way.

So, how do you discover these values? These are some of the things I would like to share with you in the following pages.

C. On the Importance of Having Goals in Life

Throughout the course of your life, Colleen, you will read about and hear many people talk about how important it is to have goals in life. In fact, it's a very popular topic for people who write a lot of self-help books. These writers often encourage people to have what they call long range goals as well as short term goals. Then, they will even encourage people to develop a detailed plan and guide you through a step by step process so that you can achieve your goals.

These kinds of books can be very helpful and are often connected to some dimension of life—like how to become more successful in your career, how to achieve some financial goal or how to become happier in your life. These books are often very practical and concrete and can be beneficial to all of us.

Having goals in life, Colleen, can be very helpful because they can help you prioritize what is really important in your life at any given time. In a sense, they can stretch you to achieve something that you might not have thought about. Goals can also have a way of leading you beyond what you thought possible. As Emily Dickinson said, "I dwell in possibility."[5] However, your goals should also be practical and realistic; otherwise they can lead to frustration and possibly depression.

Although this may sound very simplistic, Colleen, I think the most important goal you should have in life is to go to heaven—to see God and to spend eternity with Him and all your loved ones. To always have this goal in the forefront of your life can be a roadmap for the way you live your life. Jesus said: "what does it profit a person if they gain the whole world and lose their soul in the process?" By always keeping this goal in mind allows you the freedom to develop other goals in relation to this primary one.

John Henry Newman, the man I wrote my doctoral dissertation on, once wrote: "to live is to change, and to be perfect is to have changed often."[6] Another thing to remember about goals is that they can—and probably will change as you go through life. Your goals might change because you will be changing and growing and it's important to understand this and to know that this can be good thing. For example, you might have certain goals in mind

5. Dickinson, *Poems of Emily Dickinson*, 466.

6. Newman, *Development of Doctrine*, 100.

with regard to your career at one time in your life, but later—for a variety of reasons—you might want to do something else. So, you begin a process of discerning what you might want to do next and set new goals to achieve those results. In other words, be flexible with your goals because this can show growth within yourself. As you live your life, you will change in a variety of ways and hopefully these changes will bring you more growth and happiness.

D. On the Importance of Choices

Many years ago, in the 1970's, I was working on my doctorate in theology at Catholic University of America in Washington, DC. In one of my classes on ethics and virtues in life, I remember participating in a very heated classroom discussion on how a person finds meaning in their life and the impact that living a virtuous life can have on a person's psychological and spiritual development. Many students had a variety of opinions. After sharing our ideas, my professor taught us something that I have never forgotten and have often thought about. His main point was that it is our *choices* in life that define us. It is our *choices* that determine the kind of person we will become. Not our pious thoughts or good feelings but our choices. Not what we say but how we act based on the choices we make in life. "Anyone can talk a good game," he said. "But it takes courage and commitment to live out our lives in a certain way and this leads to a meaningful and happy life."

The kinds of choices you make, Colleen, will have a huge impact on your life. In my career as a therapist for over thirty years, I have seen this reality happen on a regular basis. Many of my clients have struggled to make choices that they feel are right for them, sometimes with great difficulty and personal sacrifice. Often, the impact of these choices is huge. On the other hand, I have also had some clients over the years who made very poor decisions. Sometimes, these clients were coming to counseling to try and understand why they had made such poor choices because at the time I was seeing them, some aspect of their life was not working very well. As we worked together and they gained insight into their own behaviors, they would often see the poor choices they had made and work hard to change them. Again, the impact of their choices was huge.

One of my favorite writers is Henri Nouwen. In his book, *Bread for the Journey,* he reflected on the importance of choices in our lives. Here is what he said:

> Choices. Choices make the difference. Two people are in the same accident and severely wounded. They did not choose to be in the accident. It happened to them. But one of them chose to live the experience in bitterness, the other in gratitude. These choices radically influenced their lives and the lives of their families and friends. We have very little control over what happens in our lives, but we have a lot of control over how we integrate and remember what happens. It is precisely these spiritual choices that determine whether we live our lives with dignity.[7]

Sometimes, we might think that the small decisions we have to make each day or the insignificant choices that come before us really don't matter very much. But it is important to remember that *every* choice we make is helping to shape the kind of person we are becoming. Each choice is a piece of the puzzle.

E. Live Authentically

Some years ago, I was leading a retreat Colleen, and in one of our sessions I asked the participants to take a sheet of paper and make two lists of twenty-one values that were important to them. On the first list, they were to rank these values according to what was most important to them in their work, and then on the second list to rank them according to what was most important to them personally. The list included values such as admiration, control, wisdom, competence, compassion, happiness, fame, success, power, love, and kindness.

7. Nouwen, *Bread for the Journey,* 13.

It was interesting to discover that none of those who participated in this exercise made two identical lists, and often the two lists were strikingly different. Kindness, for example, might be number two on someone's list of personal values and number fifteen on their list of desirable work values. Competence might be someone's number one professional value and come in dead last on their personal list. Many people were dismayed to discover that they lived in one way and believed in quite another. This task had made them consciously aware of this difference for the first time. As we discussed these results, a surprising number of people said that they did not think that it was possible to both live and work by the values that were personally important to them. As one man put it, "life diminishes you." But, as another person said, "only with your permission."

What was true for these retreatants, Colleen, is probably true for all of us. The experience of sacrificing authenticity and integrity is one that many people struggle with on a daily basis. Over the years, numerous people have told me in a variety of ways that they felt they could not be authentic out of fear of rejection or some other form of loss or because they find themselves living and working with people who see things very differently than they do. They have become invisible in order to survive or maintain the status quo. However, when we don't live authentically with ourselves, something begins to erode inside of us. We may survive, but we will never be whole or fully alive.

Many people these days talk about the high level of stress that they experience. But perhaps losing integrity with yourself is the greatest stress of all, far more hurtful to us than competition, time pressures, or lack of respect. Our vitality is rooted in our integrity. Becoming separated from our authentic values weakens us. This may be why, when people's lives are challenged by a serious illness and they instinctively begin to gather their strength, their values are often among the first things that change.

It is difficult, Colleen, to live authentically, to be a person of integrity. Most of us wear masks. We may have worn them for so long that we have forgotten that we have put them on. Sometimes, our culture may even try to demand that we wear them. Many of us have learned to cover over what is most authentic in ourselves in order to protect ourselves or gain the approval of others. We may have lived this way for so long that we have lost our authentic self. It is important in life, Colleen, to understand what masks we wear that cover over who we truly are and to let go of the life long roles and self expectations that we have assumed. These are ways of living that are not genuinely our own.

When I first met Kathy, her psychology practice was barely surviving. She shared offices with a group of physicians, and desperate to be accepted and work under what she perceived as the umbrella of their credibility, she took whatever crumbs fell from their professional table. Hers was the smallest office in the complex and hers was the only name not listed on the office door. It was obvious from the beginning how dedicated and gifted a therapist she was. However, this compromising attitude troubled me, although I didn't say anything about it at the time. But Kathy felt validated by the association and she was convinced that she needed referrals from the doctors in order to have clients.

Kathy was a shy person, a little apologetic and sometimes hesitant in trying to find the right words in a conversation. She was also just the slightest bit clumsy. However, all this actually made her very endearing. You felt somehow at home with her and safe. Her clients loved her.

One day she told me she was moving from her present office. Although I was pleased, I asked her why she had decided to leave. "They don't have wheelchair access," she said. I guess I looked surprised so she went on to say that she had not told me everything about herself. She continued to tell her story and said that years ago when she was young, she had a very serious stroke and was not expected to recover. "I was astonished," I said. "I had no idea." She replied, "nobody does." I went on to ask her why she had kept this part of her life a secret. Almost in tears, she said that for years she had felt damaged and ashamed. "I wanted to put it behind me," she said. "I thought if I could be seen as normal I would be more than I was." And so she guarded her secret closely. Neither her colleagues nor her clients knew. She had felt certain that others would not refer to her or want to come to her for help if they knew. However, she was no longer sure this was true.

"So what do you plan to do now?" I asked her. She looked down at her hands in her lap. "I think I will just be myself," she told me. "I will see people like myself. People who are not like others. People who have had strokes and other brain injuries. People who can never be normal again. I think I can help them be whole." Over the past six years, Kathy has become widely known for her work. She has been honored by several community groups and interviewed in newspapers. She often speaks on these kinds of topics and consults for businesses and hospitals. The many people she has helped refer others to her. Her practice is thriving. Her own name is on the door. All Kathy needed in order to be authentic was the courage to truly be herself.

There is something very appealing about a truly authentic person, Colleen. Maybe this is because we don't meet this type of person very often. An authentic person doesn't have to play a role, wear a mask, or pretend to be someone else. They are simply themselves and are comfortable with that. Moreover, an authentic person is not selfish, not focused on oneself, and doesn't want to make oneself the center of attention. They don't desire to become better known. In fact, one doesn't even need to be successful in the eyes of the world.

Authentic people are secure in themselves, comfortable in their own skin. They don't allow jealousy, ambition, or pettiness to interfere with how they relate to others. There is no whining, no resentment, no anger, no bitter claim to feeling entitled in any way. Feeling secure in themselves, they allow and encourage others to be who they truly are.

Brian Moore's novel, *The Lonely Passion of Judith Hearne*, is a story about a woman who loses her authenticity and then slowly finds it again. She lived in Dublin, Ireland, and in many ways is a very gifted woman. Healthy, bright, attractive, a respected teacher, comfortable financially, and solidly connected to her family and a number of trusted friends, she is both loved and respected.

However, there is one problem. She is approaching menopause, is unmarried and without children, and both her biology and psyche are consciously and unconsciously reminding her that her biological clock is running out!

Without fully realizing it, Judith becomes desperate. Everything in her life—her health, her job, her family, and her friends—begins to count for nothing in the face of the fact that what she really wants, a husband and children, is denied her. A great restlessness begins to grow within her, and in that unconsciously desperate state, she meets a man, an American, with whom she falls in love. The man, however, is not interested in her romantically and is pursuing the relationship only because he thinks she has money and that they might open up a restaurant together.

One night, after a date, Judith takes the initiative. She proposes marriage to the American. But he rejects her offer, telling her the truth of his intention. Judith goes on an alcoholic binge, has a nervous breakdown, and ends up in a church, cursing at God. She is taken away to a hospital where she receives good care and eventually recovers.

Shortly before she is to be released from the hospital, she receives a visit from her American friend, the man who had previously rejected her. He arrives in her room contrite, carrying a dozen roses, telling her he has been wrong, and proposing marriage. After thinking about this for a few minutes, she hands the roses back to him with these words:

> Thank you, but no thank you. I am not interested in marrying you and, to tell you why, I need to tell you a story. When you are a little girl, you dream of the perfect life you will have. You will grow up to have a beautiful body, meet the perfect man, marry him, have wonderful children, live in a wonderful home in a wonderful neighborhood, and have wonderful friends. But . . . as you get older and that dream doesn't happen, you begin to revise it, downwards. You scale down your expectations and begin to look for someone to marry who doesn't have to be so perfect . . . until you get so desperate that you would marry anyone, even if he's common as dirt! Well,

> I learned something by losing myself and then re-finding myself; I learned that if I receive the spirit for who I am, it doesn't matter whether I am married or unmarried, I can be happy either way. My happiness doesn't depend upon somebody outside of me, but upon being at peace with what's inside of me.[8]

The story has a redemptive ending with her leaving the hospital, strong and happy again, making a paper airplane out of the man's business card and floating it out of the cab window.

Authenticity is an ongoing process, Colleen, a dynamic happening over time that requires our ongoing attention. Although Judith lost hers for a period of time, she regained it and became stronger because of her struggle.

Another person, a colleague of mine, described his own experience of staying true to himself by thinking of his life as an orchestra. Reclaiming his authenticity reminds him of that moment before the concert when the concertmaster asks the oboist to sound an A. At first there is chaos and noise as all the parts of the orchestra try to align themselves with that note. But as each instrument moves closer and closer to it, there is a moment of rest, of home coming. That is how it feels to me, he said. I am always tuning my orchestra. Somewhere deep inside me there is a sound that is mine alone, and I struggle daily to hear it and tune my life to it. Sometimes there are people and situations that help me to hear my note more clearly; other times, people and situations make it harder for me to hear. A lot depends on my commitment to listening and my intention to stay coherent with this note. It is only when my life is tuned to my note that I can play life's mysterious and holy music without tainting it with my own discordance, my own bitterness, resentment, agendas, and fears. I thought this was a good image, Colleen, to understand what authenticity is all about.

Deep inside, our authenticity sings to us whether we are listening or not. It is a note that only we can hear. Eventually, when life makes us ready to listen, it will help us find our own way home.

8. Moore, *The Lonely Passion of Judith Hearne*. This is a paraphrase which tries to capture and summarize an essential part of this book.

F. The Beauty of Butterflies

Maybe one of the most difficult things to learn in life, Colleen, is that so many things in our lives are out of our control. And so, learning to accept the things in our lives that we can't control or change is extremely difficult and challenging. This is why the Serenity Prayer has always been a favorite of mine. "Lord, grant me the serenity to accept the things in life I can't change, to change the things I can, and the wisdom to know the difference."

There can be many dimensions of life that we can't control and these can certainly test our ability to accept life as it is given to us. In over thirty years in my counseling practice, I have seen this lived out by so many people in different ways. One of the interesting things I have discovered, Colleen, is that the more important the issue is to us, the more difficult acceptance will be. For example, if we don't like something a person is doing but the issue is not very important to us, then eventually it will become easier to accept if we can't change it. However, if the issue is something that is very important to us, then the struggle to accept it becomes all the more difficult.

In my own life, there have been a number of issues that have been very difficult for me to accept. Allow me to mention two of them. The first one happened when Andrew was stillborn. Accepting this seemed overwhelming at first for both Mom and myself. The pain and anguish of losing him seemed insurmountable. It was certainly something that we had no control over and couldn't change. It was something that we had to learn to accept. Fortunately, with the help of others, we became involved with an organization called Compassionate Friends which initially helped us emotionally. However, I don't believe anymore that you ever really get over this kind of loss. You simply try to grieve, to cope as best you can and move forward.

I have come to believe, Colleen, that grieving any loss, like losing a child, is a process that involves acceptance which is never easy. However, on reflection, I think that losing Andrew helped me as a therapist because grief counseling became one of the major focus points in my career. Another thing that helped Mom and me cope with our loss has been talking with each other about it and visiting your brother's grave. Although it happened so many years ago, we have quietly cried at times about losing him, and that has been healing. And finally, for me, an interesting phenomenon has happened which I don't really understand, but it has helped me cope with the loss. Over the years, butterflies have become important to me. For some reason, they have come to represent Andrew's presence. It has been amazing the times and circumstances in which I have seen a butterfly fly by or settle close to me on a blossom, and it instantly brings his presence to me. This has been comforting to me—almost like a way of staying connected, staying in touch. It's probably all just in my mind, but it has helped me.

The other reality that has been very difficult to accept and change is the fact that you are gay. This has been an ongoing struggle for me. At first, I wasn't going to write about this, but then I thought, if I didn't, I wouldn't be true to myself or honest with you. It is a major part of who you are, so I think it's important for me to talk about it.

Coming to accept this reality has been a long and difficult journey for me and one which I would like to share with you. Some years ago, when you initially shared with me that you thought you might be gay, it was devastating. I must say that I guess my emotions were all over the place. In the beginning, I think I was in denial. I hoped that it wasn't true and kept hoping that eventually you would discover that you were heterosexual. I felt upset, hurt and disappointed I guess. I think I was angry too—not at you for being gay—but angry that it had to be this way. But all along, I knew that I didn't want this reality to hurt or define our relationship.

Some time later, when you confirmed that you were gay, Mom and I struggled to integrate this new reality into our lives. I knew that this was something I had no control over and would have to learn to accept. At this time, I also had a lot of fear for you. Initially, I thought you might be somewhat young and naive about the spoken and unspoken prejudice you might experience because of being gay. I was afraid for you and worried about how you would cope with this if you experienced this kind of prejudice in your life. Finally, in struggling with my emotions about all of this, I came to feel that it was like a kind of death for me. The best way I can describe it is to say that it felt like a death to some of the dreams I had for you—the death of seeing you fall in love with a guy who would become our son-in-law. The death of having a lovely wedding, the death of having and loving grandchildren, the death of many happy family celebrations. I guess this is what most parents hope for their child. Since then, I have come to understand that this was selfish on my part. It was something I wanted "for" you rather than looking at it from your perspective.

I also firmly believe, Colleen, that my faith has helped me with this process of acceptance. I have struggled to incorporate all of this into my own spiritual life and have prayed for guidance, compassion, and acceptance. I knew that the Lord would always love you unconditionally, no matter your sexual orientation. It would make no difference to Him. Why should it make a difference to me? Praying about this helped me find some peace.

It is always challenging to accept people for who they are rather than who we want them to be. This is especially true if the way in which they are different is important to us. And because this issue has been important to me, it has become more difficult to accept. But I have also come to realize that my difficulty in accepting your sexual orientation is "on me." It is really my problem rather than yours, Colleen. Above all, Mom and I want you to be happy in life. Everyone has the right to be special to someone—to love another person and to be loved in return. Your sexual orientation is only a part of who you are and there is nothing that could ever change our love for you.

I would like to share a story with you about a prince and a beggar. Every day a very wealthy prince would ride in his ornate carriage through the countryside. And each day he would pass a poor beggar sitting along the side of the road. Whenever the prince saw the beggar, he would stop and walk over to the beggar. As he approached, the beggar would hold out his hand and the prince would give him several gold coins. Then they both would go on their way. One day, as they passed each other, the prince stopped and as the beggar approached him, the prince held out his hand to the beggar first. So, the beggar reached into his little purse, took out a grain of corn and placed it in the hand of the prince. Then they both went on their way. A little while later, the beggar stopped to rest along the side of the road. He opened his purse and discovered to his amazement that in place of the grain of corn that he had given to the prince, there was a piece of gold. Then, the beggar began to cry because he wished that he had given all his pieces of corn to the prince!

So often in life, Colleen, we are like the beggar trusting in the goodness of the prince—the Lord. We approach Him with out-stretched hands for so many things and because of his love for us, He takes care of us. But sometimes, just like the prince, the Lord offers his hand to us first. It is then that we are invited to take something out of our bag of life that is difficult, to become more generous, and put it in the hand of the Lord. I believe this is what is being asked of me with this whole gay issue. I believe that I am being invited to trust Him more deeply, because no matter what happens to us in life, He is there for us. We are invited to take our pieces of corn out of our bag because we believe that in some way, He will turn each piece of corn into a piece of gold. It is that way with the mysteries and sorrows in our lives. For me, I believe that I am being asked to take this concern I have about this gay issue out of my bag of life, so to speak, and place it into his hand, trusting that somehow He will transform it into something that is good for me.

G. The Importance of "Yet"

In John Steinbeck's splendid novel, *East of Eden*, there is a scene in which a son gives his father a present that he has selected with great care and for which he has sacrificed a great deal. The father spurns it. The reader understands that the father does this because he is an emotionally wounded person who has trouble seeing his son's better qualities and also has difficulty believing that he him-self deserves a special present. But the boy, lacking the reader's perspective, doesn't understand. The message he gets is that he is not good enough, and that rejection will color the rest of his life.[9]

There are a lot of people in the world like this boy, Colleen, walking around feeling like they are not good enough, feeling disappointed in who they are and not believing they deserve to be loved. There can also be something in ourselves that causes us to think less of ourselves every time we do something wrong. It may be the result of parents who expected too much of us, or maybe teachers who took for granted what we did right and focused instead on everything we got wrong.

So often we feel we need to be perfect for other people to love us and that somehow we forfeit that love if we ever fall short of perfection. There are few emotions more capable of leaving us feeling bad about ourselves than the conviction that we don't deserve to be loved. But God doesn't stop loving us every time we do something wrong, and neither should we stop loving ourselves and each other for being less than perfect.

Several years ago, the well known author, Rabbi Harold Kushner, wrote a book entitled *How Good Do We Have To Be?* In this work, Kushner emphasizes the fact that no one is perfect. Yet many people measure themselves and others against impossibly high standards. But the result is always the same—guilt, anger, depression, and disappointment. A healthier approach, Kushner maintains, is to learn how to put our human shortcomings into proper perspective. We need to learn how to accept ourselves and others even when we and they are less than perfect.[10]

In my years as a therapist, Colleen, I have learned a number of things about perfectionism: 1) perfectionism, is found, in varying degrees, in many people. We twist ourselves into knots, doing things to gain the approval and love of others. It would be much healthier if we could let go of what people think and accept ourselves, warts and all. 2) The quest for perfection is exhausting. We need to be gentle and compassionate with ourselves, particularly

9. Steinbeck, *East of Eden*. This is a paraphrase which tries to capture and summarize an essential part of this book.

10. Kushner, *How Good Do We Have To Be?*, 4.

when we make mistakes. No one is perfect. We need to stop holding ourselves to ridiculously high standards in a quest to prove our worth to others. We are already enough. Compassion towards ourselves leads to compassion towards others. 3) Having the courage to let others see who we really are—to see the parts of ourselves that are not perfect, can be very healing. When we are our authentic selves, we end up connecting with others on a deeper level. Don't we love the company of people who are real and comfortable in their own skin?

One of my clients told me one time that she had always worked hard at being good enough. For her, it was the golden standard by which she decided what to read, what to wear, how to act, how to spend time, where to live, and even what to say. Even good enough was not really good enough for her. She said she had spent a lifetime trying to make herself perfect. When she came to see me, she was exhausted and depressed. What she needed was to simply understand that she was human. She had always feared that she would be "found out."

Always remember Colleen, that becoming more human is what lies beyond perfection. This is because perfection is only an idea. For most experts and many of the rest of us, it has become a life goal. However, the pursuit of perfection may actually be dangerous to your health. For example, the type A personality for whom perfectionism is a way of life is associated with heart disease, high blood pressure and other illnesses.

A perfectionist sees life as if it were one of those little pictures in a monthly magazine that I read. The picture is usually called "what's wrong with this picture?" If you looked at the picture carefully, you would see that the table only had three legs or the face only had one ear. The missing things are generally pretty easy to find. In a sense, I wonder why anyone would want to take satisfaction in seeing what is missing, what is wrong, what is broken.

The pursuit of perfection has become a major dimension of life for some people. Fortunately, perfectionism is learned. No one is born a perfectionist, which is why it is possible to recover. A friend once told me that he is a recovering perfectionist. He said that before he began recovery, he always experienced himself and everyone else as always falling short. Who he was and what he did was never quite good enough. The same for other people. He said that he felt like he was always sitting in judgment on life itself. Perfectionism is the belief that life is broken.

Sometimes, perfectionists have had a parent who is a perfectionist, someone who awarded love and approval on the basis of performance and achievement. Children can learn early that they are loved for what they do and not simply for who they are. To a perfectionistic parent, what you do never seems as good as what you might do if you just tried a little harder. The life of such children can become a constant striving to earn love. Of course, love is never earned. It is a grace that we give one another. Anything else is only approval.

Few perfectionists can tell the difference between love and approval. Perfectionism is so widespread in our culture that we actually have had to invent another word to go with the word love. Unconditional love, we say. Yet, all love is unconditional.

Long before Tim went to medical school, he was trained to be a perfectionist by his father. As a child, when he brought home a ninety-eight on an exam, his father responded, "what happened to the other two points?" Tim adored his dad, and his entire childhood was focused on the pursuit of the other two points. By the time he was in his twenties, he had become as much a perfectionist as his father was. It was no longer necessary for his father to ask him about those two points. Tim had taken that over for himself. It was many years before he found out that those points don't matter. They are not the secret to living a life worth remembering. They don't make you lovable or whole.

Fortunately, life offers us many teachers. One of Tim's was his good friend, David, who was an artist. One day they were talking and Tim happened to mention that his driver's license was coming up for renewal and that he needed to take a written test on the traffic laws. The DMV had sent him a little booklet. Tim studied it for days. During these days while Tim was memorizing the meaning of the white curb and yellow curb, David would try to persuade him to join him for a walk or go to a party or go out to dinner. Tim told him he couldn't take the time. He had to study. In the end, Tim received 100 percent on the test. Feeling triumphant, he rushed into David's studio shouting his good news. David looked up from his painting with an expression of great kindness. "Why," he said, "would you want to do that?"

It was not the response that Tim had expected. Suddenly, he understood that he had sacrificed a great deal to get a hundred on a test that he had only needed to pass in order to drive. He had spent hours studying for it that he could have spent in much wiser ways. He had learned many things that he did not even want to know! But Tim really felt as if he had no choice. If his father could not approve of him with anything less than 100 percent, he could not approve of himself with less than 100 percent either. Even on a written driving test.

However, this entire experience was not really about driving. It was not even about grades. It was about needing to deserve love. Fortunately, his friend David did not play by these rules. He didn't even know the game.

How freeing it is to know that we don't need to be perfect to be loved. That we don't need to get 100 percent on so many dimensions of life. Moreover, we can truly love others because they are not perfect either. In other words, it's ok to be human. And maybe this is the more difficult challenge, Colleen. Appreciating our own humanness and the humanness of others, we realize that each of us is unfinished, that each of us is a work in progress. Each of us is like an unfinished symphony. Perhaps one word in our English language that we probably don't use very often, is the word *yet*. But it is very important in understanding who we are. Maybe it would be most accurate to add the word *yet* to all our assessments of ourselves and each other. Bill has not learned compassion . . . yet. I have not developed courage . . . yet. I am not as kind as I would like to be . . . yet. It changes everything. It allows us to become less perfectionistic, less critical, less judgmental about life itself. If life truly is a journey, a process, then all judgments are provisional. We can't judge something until it is finished—even ourselves. Each of us is a work in progress. We are not finished . . . yet. No one has won or lost until the race is over.

Perfectionistic people can be profoundly judgmental about most things. What is lacking always seems so clear to them. However, this way of judging life colors a person's reactions to themselves and those around them. As a person struggles to free themselves from this way of seeing life, it allows them to grow into a place where we see the need for one another which then allows us to join together in becoming more whole.

H. Light Your Candle

Truly embracing our lives, Colleen, can be very challenging. But it is very important because it allows us to become who we are truly meant to be. In a sense, I suppose that it is easy to embrace the nice parts of ourselves but what about the parts of ourselves that we don't particularly like? What do we do with these parts?

We all need a safe place to share who we truly are and talk about what is truly important to us. Sometimes, a retreat can be helpful in doing this. In one retreat that I participated in, a sand-tray box was used and the eight people on the retreat had the opportunity to choose objects from a sand-tray room that somehow represented what was important to them in life and then to use these objects to share this meaning with each other.

Joan, a young lawyer, took part in one of these sessions. As each person seated around the sand-tray table placed the objects they had gathered into their section of the sand, I noticed that she kept something back and put it under her chair. Because the instruction was to use all the symbols you brought to the table, I had wondered why she had done this. One by one, the group members spoke about the objects they had chosen and shared how each object symbolized what was important to them. Joan listened closely and seemed deeply moved by what the others were saying. About halfway through, she began to speak about what she had put in front of her in the sand. When she finished, she fell silent for a few moments and then hesitantly told us that there was something she wanted to add that she did not want others to see. She asked us to close our eyes while she did this.

Everyone closed their eyes. In the silence, Joan reached under her chair for the object she had hidden. After a few moments, she told us we could open our eyes, and we saw that she had placed a slender white candle in a tall candlestick in the center of her part of the sand-tray. It was unlit. Just showing it to us obviously had a deep emotional significance for her. Another retreatant offered her a box of matches, and she sat holding them for a long time, unable to light the candle or even talk about it. Finally, she lit it, saying in a barely audible voice that it represented her real self. It was a touching moment, especially powerful because the candle bore a striking resemblance to her own beauty and simplicity.

One at a time, others also shared the meaning of their objects, and then the woman seated next to Joan at the table began to speak. She, too, had an unlit candle in her tray. It was short and fat. She told us that it represented her dream of being a professional and truly wanting to help others. As she spoke, instead of lighting her candle with the matches, she picked it up, reached across the low wooden boundary between her section of the table and Joan's and lit it from the flame of Joan's candle. Joan burst into tears.

Then, this woman began to apologize, saying that she had no idea why she had not used the matches and had not meant to invade Joan's sand-tray. "Oh no," Joan told her, "it's that there is usually so much cynicism and judgment among us that I never show anyone at work what really matters to me. Only my very good friends know. I am afraid that people will laugh or that they will think less of me and so I hide myself. For me, my work is holy. It is my calling. When you lit your candle from mine, I saw why it might be important to stop hiding. Perhaps I can find the courage to be who I really am. Perhaps there are others who are hiding too." There was a moment of silence, and then these two women reached for each other's hands.

Embracing our lives and becoming who we truly are meant to be requires many choices. Sometimes, these choices help us to stop hiding and enable us to become the person we are meant to be. Growing in life, Colleen, means that we are always trying to put the pieces of the puzzle of our lives together without knowing the picture ahead of time. Over the years in my counseling work, I have seen many people struggle with significant problems, deal with profound loss and grief, and gradually find new meaning from the fragments of their lives. Over time, this new meaning has proven to be transformative. It is the kind of strength that never comes to those who deny or try to run away from their pain.

I. Untying the Knots

Much of what I have tried to do as a therapist for over thirty years, Colleen, is to help people become free from what entangles them. This is so important because only people who are not enslaved by something or someone can follow their own hearts and listen to their own goodness.

There can be numerous things that keep us tied into knots. One of the most debilitating ones is fear. People can be fearful of so many things in so many different ways that they seem to be locked into them.

One of my clients had been locked in a web of fear for years when she came to see me. After listening to Deborah's fears for more than six months, I decided to try a new approach to help her cope with her fears. One day, I told her that for the next four weeks she was simply not allowed to be afraid. She looked at me with confusion, unable to imagine what I meant. Carefully, I explained to her that I had observed that her first reaction to just about everything was fear and that when people had one reaction to everything, that reaction became suspect. In short, I did not believe that all her fear was true.

Abruptly, she became angry, telling me that I was not compassionate and indeed did not understand her. "No," I said, "I believe that after all these months, I do understand you very well. This fear that has so little to do with who you truly are has gotten in the way of your growth." Calmer, she asked again what it was that I was suggesting that she do. She reminded me that she experienced fear many times every day. "I know," I told her, "and I am proposing an experiment." I suggested that whenever she felt fear that she think of it as only her first response to whatever was happening. The most familiar response, as it were. But then I encouraged her to look for her second response and follow that. "Ask yourself, 'if I was not afraid, if I were not allowed to be afraid, how would I respond to what is happening?'" She was reluctant, but she agreed to try.

At first, Deborah had been discouraged to notice how many times she experienced fear every day. But gradually, she was surprised to find that often she could step beyond her initial stab of fear with some ease, and then she had a wide variety of different reactions to the events in her life. It had never occurred to her to challenge her fear in this way before.

After a few months, she even began to wonder whether she, herself, was afraid. For the first time, she questioned if the fear that had been her life's constant companion was just a sort of habit, a knee-jerk response to life that she had learned years ago. Over the next few months, whenever she felt fear, she would stop and ask herself if it were true, looking closely to see if she really was afraid. Surprisingly, she often discovered she was not.

Over time, she found that she was not afraid to submit her work to others, not afraid to try when she was not sure she could succeed, not afraid to speak out in defense of her values, not afraid to introduce herself to someone and offer them her help, not afraid to confront an angry person. Her mother had been afraid of all these things.

Staying safe had been the most important thing in her mother's life. Slowly, Deborah came to realize that it was not the most important thing in hers. Her mother had lived a narrow and unhappy life. At the end of our sessions, she told me that "if you carry someone's fear and live by someone else's values, you may find that you have lived their lives."

Another fear that many people struggle with is fear of the unknown. This is very understandable, Colleen, because the unknown is always difficult to handle constructively. Most of us are more comfortable with what we know. Sometimes, it might be difficult to deal with the known in our lives but at least it doesn't generate the same level of anxiety that dealing with the unknown does. As the eminent family therapist Virginia Satir said, "most people prefer the certainty of misery to the misery of uncertainty."[11]

The unknown is a real part of everyone's life, Colleen. It is something that everyone struggles with. It can keep you tied in knots, afraid of trying anything new which can be very limiting in your life. It can hinder you from exploring new destinations. It can make you stay in a job that you are unhappy with, it can keep you hanging on to a relationship or a friendship when it is much better to move on. If you let it dominate your life, it can keep you from growing in a variety of ways.

It is always good to remember that when you are trying to make a decision about something new in your life, especially the more important decisions, you can always talk with someone about the issue. Sharing with someone else that you trust, bouncing your ideas off of them, can help you sort out a path to follow. And, it will keep you from becoming stuck, from becoming tied in knots, from becoming paralyzed by fear.

Finally, Colleen, always remember to face into your fears. Don't run away from them or try to hide from them. Very often, in my experience, if you do this, it will only make them worse. Facing into a fear and tackling it head on begins a process within yourself of handling it in a constructive way. Always trust yourself. Believe that you have all the capabilities to make good, healthy decisions. Then if you need to, check things out with someone you trust. Together, you can untie all the knots and find freedom.

I realize that you don't go to church regularly anymore, but it is interesting to see that in the Scriptures the apostles were often anxious and afraid. Many times, their fear was caused by the unknown. It seems as though Jesus was constantly trying to encourage them to trust him and not to worry or be afraid. One time, when Jesus got into a boat, followed by his disciples, a storm broke out over the lake. Matthew says that the storm was so violent that the waves were breaking over the boat. But Jesus was asleep. So, they went to him

11. Quoted in *The Family Networker,* 13, 30.

and woke him saying, "save us Lord, we are going down!" And he said to them, "why are you so frightened, you men of little faith?" And with that he stood up and rebuked the winds and the sea and all was calm again" (Matt 8:23–27).[12] At another time, Jesus told his disciples not to worry about your life and what you are to eat, nor about your body and how you are to clothe it. "Look at the birds," he said. "They do not sow or reap or gather into barns; yet your heavenly Father feeds them. Are you not worth much more than they are? Can any of you, for all your worrying, add one single cubit to his span of life? . . . So do not worry about tomorrow. Tomorrow will take care of itself. Each day has enough trouble of its own" (Matt 6:25–34). And similarly, in John's Gospel, Jesus tells his disciples: "do not let your hearts be troubled, or afraid" (Jn 14:27).

Even Jesus had to face his own fears. He set Jerusalem as his destination, knowing that he would be crucified there. Can we ever imagine how difficult it would be to go to a town where we know we would be killed? He allowed himself to face into his fear, but did not let the fear control him. And in the garden of Gethsemane, his anguish was so intense that he sweated blood.

It is not easy facing our fears, Colleen. Each of us can be afraid of things in our lives in our own way. Fear is an honest human emotion. We don't have to apologize for being afraid. But like Jesus and Deborah, the key is to face into our fears and not let them dominate our lives. What can help us in this regard is to allow the words of Jesus to penetrate our hearts. "Do not be afraid. It is I." "Do not let your hearts be troubled." We know that He is with us to calm our fears. If we can trust in the Lord to always be with us, we can surrender our fears to him. Surrender is like letting go and letting God. It is believing that He is always with us and stronger than our fears. In my experience, more than any single thing, fear is the stumbling block to living life gratefully. Perhaps it is only the things we fear that we wish to control. But this can be exhausting. No one can serve life and grow in a life of gratitude if they are afraid of life. Life is a process. Deborah had worked hard to understand her fears and become

12. Unless otherwise noted, Scripture quotations are from The Jerusalem Bible, available at www.usccb.org/bible.

free of them. In the end, she felt that she had a new lease on life—a new inner freedom to be who she truly was. Sometimes, it takes a long time to become free. But that doesn't matter. It may be the most worthwhile way to spend our time.

J. Live with Courage

The great English statesman, Winston Churchill, said that courage is the first of human qualities because it guarantees all the others.[13] Soren Kierkegaard, the famous existentialist philosopher, pointed out that courage isn't the absence of despair and fear but the capacity to move ahead in spite of them.[14]

The date was July 6, 1535. Sir Thomas More had been a prisoner in the tower of London for over a year. It was now time for his execution. When he came out to mount the steps to the scaffold, he said to the officials, "I pray you, Mr. Lieutenant, see me safe up and for my coming down, I can shift for myself." While he was on the scaffold, More said that he died, "the kings good servant, but God's first."[15]

Sir Thomas More (1478–1535), was an English lawyer, author, statesman and councillor to Henry VIII. More opposed the king's separation from the Catholic Church and refused to acknowledge him as supreme head of the Church of England. He also refused to acknowledge Henry's annulment from Catherine of Aragon and his subsequent marriage to Anne Boleyn. Tried for treason for refusing to take the Oath of Supremacy which would have made the king the supreme head of the English Church, he was convicted and beheaded. Sir Thomas More was canonized by the Catholic Church in 1935 and today is the patron of lawyers.

St. Teresa of Avila said, "to have courage for whatever comes in life—everything lies in that."[16] Fortunately, most of us don't

---

13. Quoted from brainyquote.com/winstonchurchill.html.

14. May, *The Courage to Create*, 3.

15. Quoted from brainyquote.com/thomasmore.html.

16. Quoted from brainyquote.com/teresaofavila.html.

need to have the kind of courage that enabled St. Thomas More to give his life for a moral principle.

We can think of courage, Colleen, in a big way—like someone risking their life to save another or perhaps first responders who are always there risking their lives to protect us. But courage is a much richer idea than this. Over the years, in my counseling practice, I have come to understand that many people are extremely courageous in a quiet, unassuming way. However, they get no press, no notoriety. But, if St. Teresa is correct in saying that having courage is important to each of us for whatever we have to face in life, then we can begin to capture the importance of this virtue.

Courage always involves a choice, Colleen. We might not ever truly understand what motivates our choices or another person's choice, but over time, the choices we make will help determine the kind of person we will become. St. Thomas More clearly made a courageous choice in his life.

Over the years, I have come to look at my counseling room as a place of refuge. A place where people can feel safe and find the courage to face their lives in a non-judgmental way. If this atmosphere can be experienced by my client, I have seen the courage of people expressed in many different ways. Here are some examples.

Consider, for a moment, the courage it requires on a daily basis, to face an illness or addiction. Or, the courage it takes "to speak the truth in love," as St. Paul said, to someone about an issue or behavior that is wrong or unhealthy when doing this might jeopardize a long time friendship. Or, in the business world, what about the courage it takes to refuse to participate in an unethical practice when it might cost a person their job. There is even a great deal of courage involved in our willingness to work on ourselves—to rid ourselves of our masks, our false selves as the spiritual writer Thomas Merton says. This kind of willingness to die to ourselves and our selfishness often requires a healthy dose of courage. Spiritual writer and psychologist Rollo May wrote, "in human beings courage is necessary to make being and becoming possible."[17] It takes courage and a lot of hard work to become who you are meant to be. Thomas Keating, a Trap-

17. May, *The Courage to Create*, 4.

pist monk and spiritual writer, expresses our calling: "the greatest accomplishment in life is to be what we are, which is God's idea of what He wanted us to be when He brought us into being. . . . Accepting that gift is accepting God's will for us, and in its acceptance is found the path to growth and ultimate fulfillment."[18]

Furthermore, we may not often make the connection between courage and personality, but in some mysterious way, I have often seen how courage is associated with our personalities. What might be an easy thing to do for some people, might require a great deal of courage from someone else. For example, an extrovert might find it easy and actually be energized by going into a room full of people they don't know, introduce themselves and carry on a conversation and truly enjoy it. On the other hand, an introvert might be able to do this, but won't particularly enjoy it or be energized by it. It can take courage for this person to make themselves walk into this type of situation.

Some years ago, one of my clients was a young business man who had recently been diagnosed with cancer. He came to see me because he was mostly concerned with how his wife would be able to manage both his illness and the possibility of his death. He described her as painfully shy and retiring, almost fragile. They had even eloped because she could not face having a public ceremony. He could not imagine how she would be able to deal with their children and with his very successful business by herself.

When I first met her, she was very much as he said. Yet as he struggled with his cancer treatments and eventually died prematurely, she underwent a remarkable change. It was she who supported him in taking risks, even calling doctors and other experts all over the country. It was she who took over more and more of his business, learning as she went. Most importantly, it was she who supported and comforted their children. Her courage, in both her personal and her business life, was as awesome as it was unexpected. By the time he died, she was running the business and afterwards continued to make a success of it alone.

18. Keating, *The Heart of the World*, 69.

A few years after her husband died, she called me for an appointment. She wanted to discuss some decisions about her children's education and ask me if he had indicated any opinions that might serve as guidance for her now. The person who came to visit me was not the woman I had met only three years before. I commented on the changes and on the remarkable strength and courage she had shown in dealing with her husband's illness and death and in making her own life. I asked her if she had known that she would be able to do the things she had done in the past few years.

"Well, no," she said. She went on to say that she had always been shy, and been labeled by others as shy from the time she was a small girl. So no one had ever challenged her and she had never challenged herself. Yet her courage and her ability to take risks had come very naturally to her. She had been surprised at first, but then she had decided that her courage was because of her shyness. She smiled and went on to say, "I was so shy that it took courage for me to say hello to someone, it took courage to go to the grocery store and to the cleaners, it felt like a risk every time I answered the telephone. It took a lot of courage just to live, to do the things that other people do without thinking every day. I guess over the years my courage just grew from being used all the time like that. And when the time came that Joe needed me so badly, when I could no longer help him and be shy, why, I guess I was ready."

In a sense, Colleen, we are all more than we know. Wholeness is never lost, it is only forgotten. Integrity rarely means that we need to add something to ourselves. Often, it is more an undoing than a doing, a freeing ourselves from beliefs we have about who we are and ways we have been persuaded to *fix* ourselves to know who we genuinely are. Even after many years of seeing, thinking, and living one way, we are able to reach past all that to claim our integrity and live in a way we may never have expected to live.

We usually look outside of ourselves for heroes and teachers. It has not occurred to most people that they may already be the role model they seek. The courage and wholeness they are looking for may be trapped within themselves by beliefs, attitudes, and self-doubt. But our wholeness exists in us now. Trapped though it may be, it can be called upon for guidance, direction, and most fundamentally, comfort. It can be remembered. Eventually, we may come to live by it.

Some years ago, I heard a story about a lady who volunteered at a shelter for abused children. One day, this lady met a boy named Billy. He had been terribly wounded and was reluctant to go beyond the security he had found in his room. The day of the Christmas party, he shrank against the pillow on his bed and refused to leave his room. "But aren't you coming to the party?" the lady asked. He shook his head. "Sure you are," said another volunteer beside me. "All you need is to put on your courage skin." His eye brows went up. He thought for a moment. "Okay," he finally said. While the lady watched, the other volunteer helped him don an imaginary suit of "courage skin," and off he went to the party, willing to risk leaving the secure place of his room. Maybe in the end, we need to be more like Billy. We need to put on our courage skin.

K. Hold on to Your Dreams

In the musical Les Miserables, Fantine, a poor young woman who is forced by circumstances to become a prostitute, sings a beautiful song entitled, "I Dreamed a Dream." It speaks about her life.

> There was a time when love was blind
> And the world was a song
> And the song was exciting
> There was a time
> Then it all went wrong
> I dreamed a dream in time gone by
> When hope was high
> And life worth living
> I dreamed that love would never die
> I dreamed that God would be forgiving
> Then I was young and unafraid
> And dreams were made and used and wasted . . .
> But there are dreams that cannot be

And there are storms we cannot weather
I had a dream my life would be
So different from this hell I'm living
So different now from what it seemed
Now life has killed the dream I dreamed[19]

I'm sure you have already discovered, Colleen, that it is not a gentle world. For many people, life is a struggle in so many ways. And these struggles can cause our dreams to die. Everyone goes through difficulties in life of one kind or another. Everyone has sorrows that they struggle with personally or professionally. And, like Fantine, everyone struggles at times not to let our dreams die—dreams about ourselves, dreams about some part of our life, dreams about some dimension of our world. We don't want to let life kill the dreams we have dreamed.

When I talk about these kinds of dreams, Colleen, I don't mean some flighty ideas or some passing thought about ourselves or some dimension of our life. It's not saying something to yourself like, "wouldn't it be nice if . . . I were more kind or more loving." Or, "wouldn't it be nice if . . . I could be happier in my job." No, this is not what I mean by holding on to your dreams. It is much more positive than that. What I am talking about here are the dreams, the ideas we have about improving some dimension of our life and then developing a plan to make that dream a reality. For example, if you have a dream, a goal, a desire to obtain a Ph.D. in your profession, then you make that a goal and develop a realistic plan to achieve it. And even though it will not be easy and there will be difficulties along the way, you stick to your plan to achieve your goal about making this kind of dream a reality. Rather than allowing the difficulties of life to kill this dream, like it did for Fantine, you work through any difficulties and persevere in your effort to achieve your dream.

19. This musical is based on the French historical novel by Victor Hugo, first published in 1862. It is generally considered one of the greatest novels of the nineteenth century.

This is what Morrie tried to share with Mitch in *Tuesdays with Morrie*. One time, Morrie asked Mitch, "what do you want to do when you get out of college?"

"I want to be a musician," Mitch said. "A piano player."

"Wonderful," Morrie replied. "But that's a hard life."

"Yeah."

"A lot of sharks. That's what I hear," Morrie said. "Still, if you really want it, then you'll make your dream happen."[20]

This is the idea, Colleen, that, if you really want something, you work hard to make your dream happen. And even though there will be difficulties and challenges along the way, you stick with it. This is the way you hold on to your dreams.

A good image of this process to reflect on might be an oyster. An oyster is soft, tender, and vulnerable. Without the sanctuary of its shell it could not survive. But oysters must open their shells in order to "breathe" water. Sometimes, while an oyster is breathing, a grain of sand will enter its shell and become a part of its life.

These grains of sand cause pain, but an oyster does not alter its soft nature because of this. It does not become hard and leathery in order not to feel. It continues on its journey to entrust itself to the ocean, to open and breathe in order to live. However, it does respond. Slowly and patiently, the oyster wraps the grain of sand in thin translucent layers until, over time, it has created something of great value in its place where it was once most vulnerable to its pain. A pearl might be thought of as an oyster's response to its pain. Of course, not every oyster can do this. Oysters that do are far more valuable to people than oysters that do not.

Sand is a way of life for an oyster. If you are soft and tender and must live on the sandy floor of the ocean, making pearls becomes a necessity if you are to live well. This process of an oyster turning a grain of sand into a pearl is like the process inside of us of turning pain into growth. And the growth that we seek is the ability to hold on to our dreams and not let them die. Our pearl is the wisdom that allows us to persevere through our sorrows and disappointments to make our dreams a reality.

20. Albom, *Tuesdays with Morrie*, 47.

4

On Finding Meaning
and Happiness in Life

WE ALL WANT TO find meaning in our lives, Colleen. It is one of the universal desires of every person. We want to know that our lives are important, that we make a difference in life. And so, how each of us searches for answers to this question will help determine the way we live. Celebrated author Victor Frankl wrote a book called *Man's Search for Meaning*. In this book, he reported that surviving the concentration camps during the second world war often depended on seeking and finding meaning. In those camps, the people who were able to maintain a sense of meaning and purpose in their suffering were better able to survive the atrocities of their daily lives than those who could not.

If we look to our culture, you can be sure that it is constantly trying to answer this question. Our culture says that the way you find meaning and happiness in life is to be successful, to climb the corporate ladder, to become more wealthy, have more friends, try to do this or that to have more fun—all of these things will help you find meaning in your life.

The problem with these approaches is that it never really works because they are focused on ourselves. It's part of the *me* culture. The way you find true meaning in your life, Colleen, is not to focus on yourself but to devote yourself to something other than yourself. Then, that will fill your life with true meaning. In the book *Tuesdays with Morrie*, Morrie talks about this idea and he tells the author, Mitch: "So many people walk around with a meaningless life. They seem half asleep, even when they're busy doing things they think are important. This is because they're chasing the wrong things. The way you get meaning into your life is to devote yourself to loving others, devote yourself to your community around you, and devote yourself to creating something that gives you purpose and meaning."[1] In another place, Morrie said: "People haven't found meaning in their lives, so they're running all the time looking for it. They think the next car, the next house, the next job. Then they find those things are empty, too, and they keep running."[2] There is certainly a lot of wisdom in these two quotes.

In another book, *The Prophet*, the author, Kahlil Gibran has another way of talking about finding meaning in our lives. He says, "you get but little when you give of your possessions. It is when you give of yourself that you truly give."[3] And there are so many ways of giving of ourselves. St. Teresa of Calcutta once said: "some give by going, others go by giving."[4] Throughout your life, Colleen, you will find many ways of giving of yourself. This is the way you will find true meaning and happiness in your life. If you keep this idea before you as you move through the years—and give of yourself—you will find your life will be filled with true meaning, happiness and peace.

It is often difficult, Colleen, to discover a healthy balance in life. We all struggle with the following kinds of questions. Am I being too hard or too easy on myself? Am I unhappy because I'm selfish? What is real growth and what is simply my ego making its demands? Where do I find that line between discipline and enjoyment? Consequently, it is rare in our culture, to find the person who has found the right balance between self-assertion and self-effacement, between egoism and altruism, between self-development and commitment, between creativity and sacrifice,

---

1. Albom, *Tuesdays with Morrie*, 43.

2. Ibid., 136.

3. Gibran, *The Prophet*, 20.

4. Quoted from brainyquote.com/motherteresa.html.

between being too hard on oneself or too easy, or between clinging dependence and unhealthy independence. In some way, finding meaning and happiness in life is all about finding the right balance.

A. On the Importance of Our Attitudes

Discovering the right balance in life and finding meaning and happiness has a lot to do with our attitudes, Colleen. This is because so much in life depends on how we see things—the attitudes we have. The writer, Marcel Proust, said that the voyage of discovery lies not in seeking new vistas but in having new eyes.[5] There is an old Carolina story I like about a country boy who had a great talent for carving beautiful dogs out of wood. Every day he sat on his porch whittling, letting the shavings fall around him. One day a visitor, greatly impressed, asked him the secret of his art. "I just take a block of wood and whittle off the parts that don't look like a dog," he replied.

Finding meaning and happiness in life can be like this. It depends on how we *see* something. If we see something in a certain way, we can become stuck. But if we struggle to see something in a different way, it can free us and gradually lead to new life. Psychologist Wayne Dyer, a popular self-help writer said: "when you change the way you look at things, the things you look at change."[6]

Learning to develop the right attitudes in your life is so important, Colleen, and can often be the difference between being constantly upset about something and finding peace within yourself. This is not to suggest that finding the right attitude is easy—only that it is important. And sometimes, as you struggle to find the right attitude about something, you will also discover a lot of growth going on inside of you.

Charles Swindoll is a pastor and spiritual writer who reflected on the importance of our attitudes. Here is what he said.

5. Quoted from brainyquote.com/marcelproust.html.
6. Quoted from brainyquote.com/waynedyer.html.

The longer I live, the more I realize the impact of attitude on life. Attitude, to me, is more important than facts. It is more important than the past, than education, than money, than circumstances, than failures, than successes, than what other people think, or do, or say. It is more important than appearances, giftedness, or skill. It will make or break a company, a church, a home. The remarkable thing is, we have a choice every day regarding the attitude we will embrace for that day. We cannot change our past. We cannot change the fact that people will act in a certain way. The only thing we do is play on the one string we have, and that is our attitude. I am convinced that life is 10 percent what happens to me, and 90 percent how I react to it. And so it is with you. We are in charge of our attitudes.[7]

Even Martin Luther King, Jr. struggled with his attitude to accept his own personal struggles in life. At one point, he said: "my personal trials have also taught me the value of unmerited suffering. As my sufferings mounted, I soon realized that there were two ways in which I could respond to my situation—either to react with bitterness or seek to transform the suffering into a creative force. I decided to follow the latter course."[8]

Your life will offer you many opportunities, Colleen, to reflect on the attitude you will have about something. Sometimes, you will be invited to modify, adjust, or change your attitude about some dimension of your life. Hopefully, as you struggle to do this, it will lead to growth and peace.

B. Cultivating a Grateful Heart

One of our neighbors has a sticker on the back of their car that says *choose to be grateful*. As I pass this car every day walking our dog, Sadie, it is a constant reminder to me of how important gratitude is in our lives. But gratitude can be difficult to cultivate. It's not that we are ungrateful. Most people want to be grateful. But how do we

7. Zuck, *Speakers Quote Book*, 28.
8. King, "Suffering and Faith," 41.

cultivate an "attitude of gratitude?" How do we develop a grateful heart, where we are not simply grateful for one thing or another, but find that our entire life is permeated with gratitude?

It's interesting to see that gratitude was clearly important to Jesus. The well known story of the ten lepers certainly highlights this. In chapter seventeen of Luke's Gospel, he writes:

> As he entered one of the villages, ten lepers came to meet him. They stood some way off and called to him, 'Jesus! Master! Take pity on us.' When he saw them he said, 'Go and show yourselves to the priests.' Now as they were going away they were cleansed. Finding himself cured, one of them turned back praising God at the top of his voice and threw himself at the feet of Jesus and thanked him. The man was a Samaritan. This made Jesus say, 'were not all ten made clean? The other nine, where are they? It seems that no one has come back to give praise to God, except this foreigner.' And he said to the man, 'stand up and go on your way. Your faith has saved you' (Luke 17:11–19).

It seems as though we are not the only ones who struggle with gratitude. In some ways, it seems hard to believe that all the lepers who had been cured would not have come back to thank the Lord. In the time of Jesus, leprosy was such a dreaded disease with so many social implications. To not come back and say thanks is almost unthinkable! And you can almost hear the disappointment in the words of Jesus, "were not all ten made clean? The other nine, where are they?"

When we reflect on this story, it is easy for us to believe that if this happened to us, we would certainly come back to say thanks. It is also easy for us to wonder why the other nine never came back. Yet, in our own lives, there can certainly be gaps in our gratitude. We can easily be people who remember to say thanks once in a while to the Lord or other people for this thing or that thing, but how can we grow in a life of gratitude so that it permeates our entire being? How can we cultivate a grateful heart?

The well known English writer G. K. Chesterton once wrote: "Nothing taken for granted; everything received with gratitude;

everything passed on with grace."[9] So, how can we receive everything with gratitude, Colleen, and pass it on with grace? This is what I mean by cultivating a grateful heart.

Abraham Joshua Heschel is a well known author and spiritual writer. He reminded people that "just to live is holy. Just to be is a blessing."[10] If Heschel is right, what keeps us from receiving life's blessings and becoming more grateful for them? What holds us back from growing in a life of gratitude? It is not always so simple a thing as a lack of time. Often, we may not recognize a blessing when it is given, or we may have ideas about life that keep us from experiencing what we already have. Or, sometimes we can become frozen in the past which can make us miss many of our blessings in the present. We may even feel entitled to what has been given to us by grace. There are many ways to feel empty in the midst of our blessings. If this is the case, it will be more difficult to cultivate a grateful heart.

You will find, Colleen, that growing in a life of gratitude and cultivating a grateful heart requires us to deepen our awareness of life. For most of us, this is not easy. It requires work. But the effort we put into this endeavor can bear tremendous fruit. There are numerous practical ways of doing this. One of the ways I have found helpful over the years is to suggest to people that they review the events of their day for fifteen minutes every evening, asking themselves three questions and writing down the answers to these questions in a journal. The three questions are: 1) what surprised me today? 2) What moved me or touched me today? 3) What inspired me today? Often, these are busy people, and I tell them that they do not need to write a great deal; the key thing is in reliving their day from a new perspective and not the amount that they write about it. Naturally, people have varying degrees of success with this process. But if they stay with it, I have seen it have a tremendous impact on a person's life. It can have a tremendous impact on yours too, Colleen. It will deepen your awareness of life, and lead to cultivating a grateful heart where you see everything as a gift.

9. Kea, *Amazed by Grace*, 164.

10. Quoted from brainyquote.com/abrahamjoshuaheschel.html.

Most of us lead far more meaningful lives than we know, Colleen. Often finding meaning and cultivating a grateful heart is not about doing things differently. It's about seeing familiar things in new ways. It's about changing our attitudes. When we find new eyes, the unsuspected blessing in our work that we have done for many years may take us completely by surprise. We will then find ourselves cultivating a grateful heart. We can see life in many ways: with our eyes, with our mind, with our intuition. But perhaps it is only those who have remembered how to see with the heart, that life is ever deeply known or served.

C. Allowing God to Hug Us

Some years ago, I read a story about a doctor who told his patient who was dying of cancer that there was nothing more that could be done for him. "I think you had better start praying," the doctor said. For this physician, prayer had become a kind of last resort, something to offer his patients when there were no more effective treatments. For him, God became his final referral.

As you know Colleen, prayer has always been an important part of my life. But over the years, my understanding of what it means to pray and how to pray has broadened. Again, I like to think that this is because I am older now, hopefully somewhat wiser, and have more life experience. In this section, I would just like to share with you, two ways of praying that I have found helpful. I have not changed in my belief about the importance of prayer but have broadened my understanding about how to pray.

Prayer is not a way to get what we want to happen, like the remote control that comes with our television set. In fact, I think that in some sense, prayer may be less about asking for things that we want or are attached to than it is about relinquishing our attachments in some way. When we pray, we don't change the world, we change ourselves. When we pray, we stop trying to control life and remember that we are a part of all life.

Sometimes, the most powerful prayers are the most simple. For me, prayer isn't simply a mental or an emotional activity. It is an experience of our "whole" being. Spiritual writer David Steindl-Rast says that anything we do with our whole heart can be a prayer.[11] T. S. Eliot wrote about a "deep center" within each of us that he called "the still point." "Except for the point, the still point, there would be no dance," he wrote.[12] Everyone possesses this center, this still point, Colleen. It is the quiet core where God's spirit dwells in us, and this can give us a different way of praying. "Do you not know . . . God's Spirit dwells in you?" (1 Cor 3:16) Sometimes we tend to forget this. Yet in some holy place within us, God lives and moves and has being (2 Cor 6:16). At this inmost center of our being, a place where we are deeply and profoundly known and loved by God, we can pray. It is here that we attach ourselves to God. But this is also where God attaches himself to us. Ultimately, as St. Hildegard of Bingen said, the still point is a love meeting, an embrace. She wrote, "God hugs you. You are encircled by the arms of the mystery of God."[13] God's hug—what a wonderful image! Maybe all we need is to allow ourselves to be hugged.

This is what I mean, Colleen, in saying that sometimes, the most powerful prayers are the most simple. With this type of prayer, what we need to do is to find quiet times, places of stillness, that allow the Lord, who is already within us, to love us. It can be such a wonderful way of praying to just sit with the Lord and allow Him to hug us.

However, this idea of just sitting in God's presence can be more difficult than we might think. We are not used to "just sitting" with God. In fact, in our fast-paced world, we are not used to sitting for anything for very long. And I think most of us are not used to praying this way. And yet, this can be so helpful in terms of praying with our whole being. There is a story about an old peasant and St. John Vianney, the Cure d'Ars. It seems as though this old gentleman would simply come into an empty church and just sit for hours. One day, the Cure d'Ars decided to ask him what he did during all these hours in church. The old peasant replied,

11. Quoted in Ross, *The Fire of Your Life*, 64.
12. Eliot, "Burnt Norton."
13. Uhlein, *Meditations with Hildegard of Bingen*, 90.

"Nothing. I just look at him and he looks at me." This old peasant understood what sitting in God's presence and allowing him to love us was all about.

The second way of praying that I have found helpful, Colleen, is learning to pray through the ordinary, everyday things of life. This might especially appeal to you because of the way you love beautiful sunsets, the beach, etc. Remember over the years, how many pictures of beautiful sunsets that you have sent me. This way of praying can be very helpful because it really flows from the Incarnation. Because God became one of us, He has made holy all of creation and realizing this can be a wonderful way of praying. Because God has become incarnate in human flesh, we find Him not simply in our formal prayers and monasteries, but in our homes, in our everyday lives. As the writer Nikos Kazantzakis puts it: "wherever you find husband and wife, that's where you find God; wherever children and petty cares and cooking and arguments and reconciliation are, there is where God is too."[14] The God of the Incarnation is more domestic than monastic.

St. John the Evangelist wrote in his first letter that "God is love and whoever abides in love abides in God" (1 Jn 4:16). When scripture affirms this, the love of which it speaks is not so much romantic love as it is the flow of life within a family. God is not "falling in love," but family, shared existence. The God of the Incarnation lives in a family, a community of shared experience. Therefore, to say that God is love is to say that God is community, family, shared existence, and whoever shares his or her existence inside of family and community experiences God and has the very life of God flow through them.

And because this is true, it can broaden the way we pray. If God is incarnate in ordinary life, then we should seek God, first of all, within ordinary life. Too often, even though we know this theoretically, practically we still look for God in the extraordinary. The God who is love and family, who was born in a barn, is a God who is found, first of all, in our homes, in our families, at our table, in sunrises, in our joys and sorrows, and even in our arguments.

14. Kazantzakis, *The Last Temptation of Christ.*

To be involved in the normal flow of life, giving and receiving, as flawed and painful as this might be at times within any relationship, is to have the life of God flow through us.

Looking at prayer in this way, Colleen, can broaden our understanding of how to pray. Participating at Mass will always be our most important prayer. Saying our prayers in whatever ways we choose to do this will continue to be an important way of praying. But so will seeing each day how God is an important part of our activities, will allow us to talk with the Lord on a continual basis. Remember, He is in the "ordinary." Seeing one of your beautiful sunsets, walking along a beautiful beach and realizing where this came from and saying "thank you" can also be a powerful prayer. Even at work, going through your various activities, and realizing that God is in the very midst of them, can be a constant way of praying.

It is said the Christian mystic St. Teresa of Avila found it difficult at first reconciling her understanding of prayer with the every day, mundane tasks of her Carmelite convent. She found it difficult to understand how washing pots and pans, sweeping the floors and folding the laundry fit into her understanding of the spiritual life. However, over time, and at some point of grace, these every day mundane tasks became for her a kind of prayer, a way in which she could stay connected to God through the day. She began to see the face of God in the folded sheets.

And so, Colleen, allowing God to hug us and seeing Him in all the ordinary activities of the day can allow you to grow in your prayer life and stay connected to God as you develop your own spirituality.

D. Eight Levels of Charity

Maimonides, a great doctor rabbi of the Jewish religion, describes what he called the eight levels of charity or ways of giving to others. Here are his descriptions of each level.

At the eighth and most basic level of giving to others, a person begrudgingly buys a coat for a shivering person who has asked him for help, gives it to that person in the presence of witnesses, and waits to be thanked.

At the seventh level, a person does this same thing without waiting to be asked for help.

At the sixth level, a person does this same thing open heartedly without waiting to be asked for help.

At the fifth level, a person open heartedly gives a coat that he has bought to another but does so in private.

At the fourth level, a person open heartedly and privately gives his own coat to another, rather than a coat that he has bought.

At the third level, a person open heartedly gives his own coat to another who does not know who has given him this gift. But the person himself knows the one who is indebted to him.

At the second level, he open heartedly gives his own coat to another and has no idea who has received it. But the person who receives it knows to whom he is indebted.

And finally, on the first and purest level of giving to others, a person open heartedly gives his own coat away without knowing who will receive it, and he who receives it does not know who has given it to him. The giving, then, becomes a natural expression of the goodness in us, and we give as simply as flowers breathe out their perfume.[15] This is very similar to what the spiritual writer John Bunyan said when he wrote: "you have not lived today until you have done something for someone who can never repay you."[16]

In the spiritual life, Colleen, we call this trying to purify our motives or reasons for doing something good for others. In a sense, we are trying to move from number eight to number one. However, suppose that we all gave to those around us as the first person does, begrudgingly offering a coat we have bought in the presence of witnesses to someone who has need and who asks us for help? If we all did this, do you think there would be more suffering or less suffering in the world than there is now?

Less suffering, I think. Some things have so much goodness in them that they are worth doing any way we can.

15. Remen, *My Grandfather's Blessings*, 86–87.
16. Quoted from goodreads.com/author/quotes/16244.johnbunyan.

E. On the Importance of Friendship

Probably one of the greatest gifts and graces in our lives are our friends. They are like special graces that the Lord gives us to help us in so many ways in our journey through life. One of my professors in graduate school at Catholic University made a statement that I have never forgotten. "Whenever our relationships are going well, there is probably nothing better but whenever our relationships don't work out, there is probably nothing worse." That statement is so true for all of us because basically we are social creatures. We are meant to be in relationship with others. We are not meant to be alone.

However, Colleen, you will discover, if you haven't already, that friendships can be a lot of things. They can be growthful, helpful in so many ways, encouraging, and freeing but also difficult, controlling and painful. That is why it is important to cultivate good friendships. You have to work at friendships with people to make them healthy and satisfying.

But maybe even before this, you will save yourself a lot of heartache by learning how to choose your friends. I am not talking about perfection here. No one is perfect and no friendship is perfect. But what I have learned in my counseling career, is that you will save yourself a lot of grief if you can avoid choosing as your friends people who have a lot of issues—people who are not well balanced emotionally or psychologically, people who are extremely needy, people who are overly clingy, or people who are controlling. Trying to make friendships grow with these kinds of people is like trying to find water in a desert—a never ending struggle and problem. Often, I have found in my work with others that people think they are going to be able "to fix" this person or that person in order to become friends but this approach usually ends up badly for both people. It's hard enough to cultivate good friendships with people who are reasonably healthy rather than trying to fix someone. That is why understanding this basic idea about friendship can be so helpful.

Another important idea about friendship is to understand ourselves and our own personalities and to look at the kinds of people that we are attracted to. We can all be attracted to unhealthy people in one way or another but if we know ourselves well enough we will be able to avoid these problems. For example, we can all be attracted to people that we want to fix or control or dominate in some way. Or, maybe we are attracted to controlling or dominating personalities ourselves or maybe to someone who we think will take care of us. But again, if you know yourself well enough, you will be able to avoid these pitfalls.

There are also different levels of friendships. It is generally believed that if we have two or three really good friends in our lives we are truly blessed. But besides these kinds of friends, we can also have other friends that we enjoy being with or doing things with even though they might not be our closest friends. In addition, we can have a certain level of friendship with people that we work with for example. These people make our work environment more enjoyable and can sometimes lead to deeper friendships.

I believe that our friends are special graces or gifts that the Lord gives us in life. To my mind, we don't just happen to run into people in our lives. Rather, the Lord is directing things so that we meet certain people and not others. And among those that we meet, some will become very good friends who help us in life in so many ways—and—we do the same for them. Good friends help us to grow and mature. They are people with whom we can share our lives—both the joys and the sorrows—people who truly know us, who we feel comfortable with and like to be with. We can't do this with everyone. That is why they are "special graces." There is a touching story about friendship in that book *Tuesdays with Morrie*. Morrie had a friend named Maurice Stein with whom he had been friends for over thirty-five years. Now, Stein was going deaf. And Morrie was getting to the point where he was unable to speak and his friend, Stein, was unable to hear. TV personality Ted Koppel was interviewing Morrie and asked him what that would be like for their friendship. "We will hold hands," Morrie said. "And there'll be a lot of love passing between us. We've had thirty-five years of friendship. You don't need speech or hearing to feel that."[17]

17. Albom, *Tuesdays with Morrie*, 70–71.

Finally, Colleen, choose your friends wisely, never take them for granted, work to cultivate them, learn to walk away from them if they are or become unhealthy and thank the Lord for them. They make our journeys through life so much more enjoyable.

F. The Shirt in the Clothes Hamper

A woman by the name of Jennifer tells the story about how her son, who was 21, had died and she left one of his shirts in the bottom of her clothes hamper as a way of remembering him. Year after year she left it there—for five years. It was one of her ways of hanging on to him. Then, one day her daughter came over and did the laundry, including her brother's shirt. When Jennifer saw his clean shirt hanging in the closet, she said she felt somewhat surprised but she didn't feel sorrow or disappointment. For her, it seemed to be the right time for the shirt to leave the dirty clothes hamper. As she reflected on the experience, she came to believe that for her it was a symbol of progress—that she was getting better and beginning to let go.

In life, Colleen, you will find that there is a tension between holding on and letting go of things. And I don't just mean material things. It can be a painful struggle and can take time. Usually, you will need to be patient with yourself. It takes time to figure out these dimensions of life sometimes. And—you will need to give yourself time in order to sort them out to make the best decision.

Perhaps there will be times in your life when you will need to hold on to someone or something for a period of time until the time is right and then you can let go. This is the way it was for Jennifer with her son's shirt in the hamper. If other people knew that she had left it in the hamper for five years, they might have thought she was a bit off! But she needed this time to work through her grief and then she could let go. And this is the way it is for all of us. We all have our own time table for working through challenging situations, and what might work well for one person will not be good for another. In Jennifer's situation, holding on to this dirty shirt served a purpose in her life. And for us, sometimes holding on serves a psychological purpose or has a particular meaning in our lives.

Holding on tends to make us feel safe, secure and in control of our lives while letting go makes us feel like we are drifting, insecure and losing control. For some, it's a personality issue and can lead to serious problems. Hoarders are probably the people at the extreme end of the spectrum but fortunately most of us are not afflicted with this kind of problem. Nevertheless, most of us struggle with this dimension of life to some degree. It's probably true to say that the areas of life we tend to cling to are personal to each one of us. Let me mention a couple of common ones that many people struggle with.

One personality or psychological issue that can become problematic for us is an excessive need for approval. Because we are social beings, it is quite normal for us to seek the approval of others who are important to us. For example, we might seek the approval of our parents, a spouse, a friend, or the boss at work. Basically, there is nothing wrong with this and it can be growthful if it's done in a good way. However, if this is done too much, it can become very debilitating. If we cling to this need for the approval of others, it can limit our ability to function freely as a person. If we live our lives needing this person or that person to approve of us, it cramps our freedom to live our lives as unique individuals. If we go through life wondering if someone agrees with us or not, it limits our ability to make our own decisions. And, if we need the approval of others too much, it can put a lot of stress on you. It can make you feel that you are in a box, trapped.

Perhaps another way of thinking about this is to ask yourself the question: "what will others think of me?" If you cannot act without them thinking well of you, then you are limiting your freedom and your ability to make free choices. However, remember what I said earlier. We don't live in a vacuum and how others think of us and our need for other's approval can be a good thing. It only becomes a problem when it becomes too dominant in our personalities. And so, letting go of the need for the approval of others and not clinging to worrying about what others think about us can bring a lot of interior freedom.

However, it is also important, Colleen, to learn to let go in life. Letting go of a situation, for example, can be a sign of growth and maturity. If you hold on too tightly or for too long, it can be detrimental to you. This is often true in relationships and career issues. In our relationships, sometimes it's difficult to let go. This seems to be especially true in friendships. We can tend to hold on to friendships for all kinds of reasons, even when we begin to suspect that we should let go of the person. And, as I noted earlier, this can take time and you will need to be patient with yourself as you move through the issues involved in order to make a decision. This can certainly be a painful process because most of us don't develop good friendships quickly or drop them easily. However, it also takes a lot of strength and courage to leave a friendship or put new boundaries on one when we realize that this would be for the best. This is when letting go can be very important. When a relationship or friendship is no longer healthy for whatever reason, or is not life-giving to you or the other person, it is time to let go and move on.

Or, how about career issues? If you are no longer happy in your career, do you simply hold on to it or let go and move on to something else? These can be very difficult decisions that can take time to resolve. Again, you will need to be patient with yourself as you sort through the issues involved and come to the best decision for yourself. And with this type of situation, there are obviously many practical dimensions you will need to consider.

One final thought about the importance of letting go. As we move through life, we can begin to cling to all kinds of "stuff." Don't become a "pack rat" Colleen. Many people hold on to so much "stuff" because they say to themselves, "some day I might need this." Learn how to let go of things, realizing that other people can use them. A wise person once said, "whatever you don't use in your life, belongs to someone else." Having this kind of attitude allows you to give to others—things like clothes, all kinds of household items or other things that many people accumulate over time. For example, as we go through life, we can accumulate a huge amount of clothes. After a while, many of us don't even wear certain pieces any more. But we keep saying to ourselves, "I might need these some day," and so we just hang on to them. Remember now, I am not suggesting that all of us don't have our favorite things that we like and hold on to, like Jennifer's shirt in the hamper. But there is a certain freedom that comes to you when you learn to share with others whatever you don't need or use anymore.

So, holding on and letting go can be important dimensions of life, Colleen. Like Jennifer, with her son's shirt in the clothes hamper, it takes all of us time to be able to move on but being able to do this can show real growth. Finally, I think the real value in all of this is that it will give you an interior freedom to grow, to develop and mature into the unique individual that the Lord wants you to be. You will not unnecessarily worry about what others think of you and you will not cling to "stuff." You will become your own person. In a word, you will be free.

G. "When You Are Walking on Thin Ice, You Might as well Dance"

Phil's grandfather was a lawyer, a judge, and a farmer. When Phil was a little boy, he and his grandfather used to go fishing at one of the little ponds on his farm. His grandfather would sit and hold his fishing pole over the water, becoming as still as the stumps that jutted up from the water. Phil usually tired of fishing fairly soon and went on to other things. One day, having given up on fishing, Phil was playing in his grandfather's old black truck when he noticed that his fishing bait was still on the seat. Phil remembered being surprised that his grandfather had been out fishing an hour or more without bait. He grabbed the bait bucket and raced over to him. "Grandaddy, how can you fish without bait?" His grandfather tilted back his hat and smiled as if he had been caught in a deep secret. "Well, sometimes it's not the fish I'm after," he said, "it's the fishing."

In other words, for Phil's grandfather, it wasn't the conquest that mattered, but being in the moment, fully in the experience, watching and waiting as life unfolded. He was letting life happen. As I have gotten older, Colleen, I realize more and more the importance of letting life happen—of living in the moment. I think part of this is true because as I have aged, I realize more realistically, that there are fewer moments left for me. This is not to be understood in a morbid sense of any kind. Rather, it's an acknowledgement of the fact that I have fewer days remaining now and need to make the most of them. I wish I had understood this idea when I was younger, but maybe it is only something you realize as you grow older. Perhaps it's part of the wisdom of aging. In any event, I can remember when I was younger, that time seemed to go so slow for me. I often found myself looking forward to the next fun thing that I was going to do, or maybe the next holiday or vacation. I found it difficult to "live in the moment," to just enjoy the fishing. As I look back on these years, I wish there had been someone who would have emphasized to me the importance of this idea of living in the moment. This is not to fault anyone. I'm sure there were people in my life who probably tried to teach me this kind of thing. I was probably just too young to hear it. Now, I regret that. Because of this, I hope that you will come to understand, Colleen, the importance of letting life happen—of living in the moment. If you can do this, it will enrich your life as you live each day and allow you to appreciate each precious moment that you have.

Of course, letting life happen and living in the moment, doesn't mean that we resort to futile resignation. It doesn't mean that we don't have goals and aspirations for the future. Rather, it means giving up our need to manipulate and control, to "bait" all the events and minutes around us. We can relax and relate to life with a faithful knowing that if we cease to act, life itself will not cease. In fact, it may grow full.

Carl Jung expressed it like this: "the art of letting things happen, action through non-action . . . became for me the key, opening the door to the way. We must be able to let things happen to the psyche. For us, this actually is an art of which few people know anything."[18]

18. Jung, *Commentary on Richard Wilhelm's The Secret of the Golden*

Meister Eckhart, the mystic whose fourteenth century writings are full of insights for our time, also wrote about letting life happen. He called it being in "true poverty."[19] Emptied of the need to achieve, a person could be free to wait in the moment. It was, he conceded, the highest way of being. Connecting this idea to the spiritual life, Eckhart believed that in learning this way of being we could begin to experience God as the newest thing there is. In waiting, we find, perhaps for the first time, God new and immediate in every moment, not something "out there" to be grasped some other time.

Over the years, I have seen the power of taking this kind of an unconditional relationship to life—to let life unfold rather than trying to manipulate and control it. Many of my clients also seem to have gradually found their way to this viewpoint on life.

When people begin to develop this kind of attitude, Colleen, they seem to become intensely alive, intensely present, and gradually more joyful. Their losses and suffering do not cause them to reject life, do not cast them into a place of resentment, victimization, or bitterness. As one person put it, "I have let go of my preferences and am living with an intense awareness of the 'miracle of the moment.'" Or, in the words of another client, "when you are walking on thin ice, you might as well dance."

H. Sway with the Wind

Trees look strong compared with the wild reeds in the field. But when the storm comes, the trees are uprooted, whereas the wild reeds, while moved back and forth by the wind, remain rooted and are standing up again when the storm has calmed down.

Flexibility is a great quality, Colleen. When we cling to our own positions and are not willing to let our hearts be moved back and forth a little by the ideas or actions of others, we may easily be broken. Being like wild reeds does not mean being "wishy-washy."

Flower, 93.

19. Fox, Breakthrough, 213.

It means moving a little with the winds of time while remaining solidly anchored in the ground. A humorless, intense, opinionated rigidity about current issues for example, might cause these issues to break our spirits and end up making us bitter people. It's important to be flexible while being deeply rooted.

Being flexible while remaining rooted can be challenging, Colleen. But it can be important in finding happiness in your life. What happens when we are flexible is that it moves us out of a win or lose situation. It allows us to avoid seeing life in an adversarial way and moves us into a powerful kind of openness. From such a position, we can then make a greater commitment to life. Not only the pleasant or comfortable parts of our lives, or our own idea of life, but all life. Seeing life in this way allows us to understand that playing the game is more important than winning or losing. As I previously said, it's like being the fisherman who sometimes is not so much interested in catching fish as he is in simply fishing.

St. Ignatius of Loyola, the founder of the Jesuits, wrote about the importance of a term that he called "indifference." For Ignatius, this was part of the process in which we try to discover the will of God for our lives. He thought that if we could become indifferent to our own preferences or desires, then we would be more open to what God wants of us. In a sense, being flexible is like this. It allows us to move beyond a place of outcomes. It doesn't mean that we don't have preferences or desire certain outcomes in situations. Rather, it allows us to move to a place of freedom, even anticipation. Decisions made from this perspective are life-affirming and not fear driven.

To the degree that we can relinquish our personal preferences about life, we free ourselves from win/lose thinking and the fear and anxiety that feeds on it. An adversarial position is generally not the strongest position in life. Freedom may be a stronger position than control. It is certainly a stronger and far wiser position than fear.

However, there can be a fundamental paradox here, Colleen. In a sense, the less we are attached to life, the more alive and joyful we can become. The less we have preferences about life, the more deeply we can experience and participate in life. This is not to say that I don't prefer a cinnamon bagel to a blueberry muffin. It is to say that I don't prefer a cinnamon bagel so much that I am unwilling to get out of bed unless I can have a cinnamon bagel, or that the absence of a cinnamon bagel ruins my whole day. Embracing life may be more about tasting than it is about either a cinnamon bagel or a blueberry muffin. More about trusting one's ability to take joy in the newness of the day and what it may bring. More about adventure than having your own way.

5

On Becoming a Blessing to Others

THERE IS A WONDERFUL book, Colleen, entitled *My Grandfather's Blessings,* by Rachel Remen, which I hope you will have a chance to read sometime. It talks about this idea of "being a blessing" to others in our lives. When you look at your life in this way, it gives you a way of focusing each day. It gives you a way of going about your day which gives everything in your day meaning.

In a sense, living each day allows you to learn how to become a blessing. Sometimes, we might not think much about our life in this way. There are so many other daily distractions—like jobs, family, friends, finances, having a good time, etc.—that consume us. But if our overall focus is to be a blessing to others today, you will find many opportunities where this might be possible.

What does it mean to be a blessing to others? I think basically it means to become more aware each day of how you can go out of yourself to be good to others. It means not focusing on yourself. It means becoming more and more aware each day of how you can be present to others in their needs. And this can be very difficult to do because most of us are focused on ourselves. We can become more and more concerned with our own needs, wants and desires rather than being attuned to what is going on around us.

It seems to me that becoming a blessing to others begins with awareness. It starts with the way we "see" things. It means opening our eyes each day to what is happening around us. It means taking our blinders off to be open to what is happening to us each day. It means living each day with a purpose. Whenever we can see more clearly, we will find many opportunities opening up before us to be a blessing to others.

Becoming a blessing to others can take many forms, Colleen, and you don't need money to do it. However, sometimes, it might involve money in some way. For example, you might have an opportunity to give something to a poor person. Maybe you can help pay an electric or water bill or buy groceries for someone. Or, if you become wealthy, you might be able to use your money in a philanthropic way—to do things for others which can have a greater and more lasting impact for many people. However, you will probably find that being a blessing to others often involves being generous with your time, your talents, your skills, or your experience. Being willing to share these parts of yourself with others often requires a lot of "giving" on your part. Giving of your time and talents to help others, giving of yourself in so many different ways, opens the possibility of being a blessing to others each day. Some of the following reflections will try to make this more concrete.

A. Live with Compassion

What do you think it means, Colleen, to live with compassion? I think the answer becomes clear when we look at the word "compassion," which literally means "with" (com-) "suffering" (passion). To have compassion is to suffer with. It is not a feeling of detached pity but sharing the pain with someone else. Compassion allows us to have empathy for another person. It means to relate to other people in such a way that we see others not as strangers but as part of us. This relatedness allows us to walk with them in their deep and wounded places.

Compassion actually begins with the acceptance of what is most human in ourselves, what is most capable of suffering. When we pay attention to our own capacity to suffer, we can uncover a simple and profound connection between our own vulnerability and the vulnerability in all others. Experiencing this allows us to find an instinctive kindness toward life which is the foundation of all compassion and genuine service.

After a dozen years, Alzheimer's disease had virtually destroyed Linda's brain, erasing her memories and with them all of her sense of who she was. Confined to a nursing home, she was adrift and frightened, given to pacing back and forth in a seemingly endless fashion filled with a nameless anxiety. Such repetitive pacing is common in people at the last stages of this disease, almost as if they are being driven to search for something hopelessly lost.

All the staff's efforts to ease her fear had failed. For a long time, she was at rest only when she slept, and her unending movement had caused her to become painfully thin. Then one day, quite by accident, as she passed the full-length mirror that hung to the left of the door to the courtyard, she caught sight of her own reflection in the glass. Becoming still for the first time in many months, she stood before it, fascinated, an odd expression on her face. She looked as if she had just met a friend from long ago, someone whose face was vaguely familiar but whose connection to oneself cannot be recalled.

As a result of her disease, Linda had not spoken in many months. But drawn to the image in the mirror for reasons long forgotten, she began to speak to it in a language all her own. Day after day, she would stand and talk to the woman in the mirror for hours on end. It made her calm.

The nurses welcomed this new behavior with relief. Her endless pacing and anxiety had made her very difficult to care for. Accustomed to much random senseless behavior on the part of their patients, they paid little further attention to how she now spent her time. But her doctor saw this differently. Every day on his rounds, he would stop at the mirror and spend some time with this patient. Standing next to her, he too would talk to the woman in the mirror with his usual kindness and respect. Once, at the end of one of his longer chats with Linda's reflection, he was deeply moved to notice that Linda had tears in her eyes. The nurses were deeply moved as well. Unable to cure his patient's brutal disease, this true physician instinctively strengthened her last connection to herself with his simple presence and validated her worth as a human being.

For Linda, who saw herself in the mirror, it was like meeting someone she had known a long time ago. Gradually, she was able to speak to herself in the mirror in a language all her own. It was like coming home to herself.

This physician had an instinctive kindness toward life which enabled him to be compassionate. And this is so often true in our own lives as well. Compassion flows from how we "see" something in life. No matter whether it is a person or a situation, if we see it with an instinctive kindness, it will lead us to be compassionate. Or, on the other hand, if we see a person or a situation in a harsh or critical way, it will often lead us to be judgmental and unkind.

The spiritual writer Meister Eckhart was adamant that compassion was the aim of all spiritual growth. "If you were in ecstasy as deep as that of St. Paul and there was a sick man who needed a cup of soup, it were better for you that you returned from the ecstasy and brought the cup of soup for love's sake."[1]

Once divine compassion takes hold of us, Colleen, we can never be the same again. We are compelled to suffer with, wait with, cry with those around us. We want to take the pain out of those who are homeless, the hungry, the abused, the rejected, the poor, the lonely, the sick, the grieving, the fragmented, the worn down, the defeated, and the oppressed as much as we can. We do it for no reason except that compassion asks it.

Meister Eckhart also said that "love has no why."[2] We can't always separate our motives and respond purely from love. There can often be hidden agendas that grow out of the little game we play of "what's in it for me." Yet real compassion flows from God dwelling within us—from plentitude, not ego or neediness. Such compassion is always born from within, not imposed or mandated from without.

One time, the director of an adolescent clinic in New York City was asked how he could continue his work year after year

1. LeShan, *How to Meditate*, 92.
2. Fox, *Breakthrough*, 206.

when the kids he saw had so many social problems that nothing he did could make a difference. "Why, no," he replied with conviction. "With kids like these, everything I do makes a difference." It all depends on your perspective, Colleen. It all depends on your attitude and the way you see things.

We know that Jesus was walking, talking compassion. Many stories in the New Testament attest to this. One time, he told his disciples, "be compassionate as your father is compassionate" (Luke 6:36). As we become more compassionate, we become more like Christ, showing an uncanny interest in the poor, the excluded, the disenfranchised, the "least of my brothers." Then, we find ourselves sitting by our Samaritan well, more interested in breaking down barriers than in religious "do's and dont's." We wrap a towel around our waist and serve one another. We come to the rescue of others, like Jesus with the adulterous woman about to be stoned, as we try to bind up the wounds around us and do our small part to create community and justice for everyone.

B. Always Strive to Take the Pain Out of Things

Back in the 1980's Colleen, there was a musical entitled *The Human Comedy*. It was the story of a teenager who was growing up in poverty in an inner city with crime all around him. He just couldn't understand why life had to be so difficult. Why did people have to struggle so much? Why was there so much suffering and sorrow and violence all around him? As he pondered these questions, he got on a bus and rode all night around the city, crying. His mother was panicking because he hadn't come home. Finally, in the morning, he came back home and began talking to his mother about all of this. After patiently listening to his questions, she told him:

> It was pity that made you cry. . . . Pity, not for this person or that person who is suffering, but for all things—for the very nature of things. Unless a man has pity, he is inhuman and not yet truly a man, for out of pity comes a bond which heals. Only good men weep. . . . There will always be pain in things. . . . Knowing this does not mean that a man

shall despair. The good man will seek to take the pain out of things. The foolish man will not even notice it except in himself. And the evil man will drive pain deeper into things and spread it about wherever he goes.[3]

Besides our individual sorrows and suffering, Colleen, there is also a collective suffering that is difficult to understand. There is so much pain in the world and in our society to which there are no easy answers. It can evoke a level of compassion that can be overwhelming. It can also make us feel helpless. We might think that compared to the size of the problem, what we do means very little. But this is simply not the case. When it comes down to it, no matter how great or how small the need, we can only bless one life at a time.

Another example of this level of suffering is exemplified in a story I read some years ago. In the 1990's, a psychologist who lived and practiced in New York City decided to attend a two-day professional workshop based on several short films of one of Carl Jung's last pupils, the great Jungian dream analyst Marie-Louise von Franz. Between the showing of these films, a distinguished panel consisting of the heads of two major Jungian training centers and Carl Jung's own grandson responded to written questions from the audience sent up to the stage on cards.

One of these cards told the story of a horrific recurring dream in which the dreamer was stripped of all human dignity and worth through Nazi atrocities. A member of the panel read the dream out loud. As he listened, the psychologist began to formulate a dream interpretation in his head, in anticipation of the panel's response. It was really a no-brainer, he thought, as his mind busily offered his symbolic explanation for the torture and atrocities described in the dream. But this was not how the panel responded at all. When the reading of the dream was complete, Jung's grandson looked out over the large audience. "Would you all please rise?" he asked. "We will stand together in a moment of silence in response to this dream." As the audience stood for a minute, the psychologist waited impatiently

---

3. Smith and Pryce, *Reading for Power*, 171, quoting from the book by William Saroyan on which the musical was based.

for the discussion that he was certain would follow. But when they sat again, the panel went on to the next question.

The psychologist simply did not understand this at all, and a few days later he asked one of his teachers, himself a Jungian analyst, about it. "Bob," his teacher said, "there is in life a suffering so unspeakable, a vulnerability so extreme that it goes far beyond words, beyond explanations and even beyond healing. In the face of such suffering, all we can really do is bear witness so no one need suffer alone."

In his book, *Night*, famous author and concentration camp survivor Elie Wiesel wrote about this kind of collective suffering with his horrifying childhood experiences in a Nazi concentration camp. Having gone without food and drink for three days, thousands of Jews were driven out of their barracks at dawn into a thickly falling snow and herded into a field. Forbidden to sit or even move very much, they stood in line until evening, waiting for a train that would take them deeper into Germany. The snow drifted in a layer on their shoulders.

Finally, their thirst became intolerable. One man suggested that they eat the snow, but the guards would not allow them to bend over. The person in front of that man agreed to let him eat the snow that had accumulated on the back of his shoulders. That act spread through the line until there, in a frozen field, what had been individuals struggling with their separate pain became a community sharing their suffering together.[4]

A compassionate heart understands that we will survive as a human family only as we are willing, one by one, to become a place of nourishment for our brother and sister. We will survive as we cease being individuals struggling alone with our sorrows and instead become a community sharing our sorrows in a great collective act of compassion.

Closer to home, so to speak, but still very much another example of collective suffering, is what I experienced every week when I was a volunteer at the Franciscan Center in a very poor section of downtown Baltimore. In the face of the sorrows of these

4. Wiesel, *Night*, 109.

people, I must admit that I sometimes ask myself why I am doing this? In the long run, what difference is this going to make for so many people who suffer every day with overwhelming sorrows? Then, I remember what Jesus told his disciples in Matthew's Gospel: "For I was hungry and you gave me food; I was thirsty and you gave me drink; I was a stranger and you made me welcome; naked and you clothed me, sick and you visited me, in prison and you came to see me. . . . I tell you solemnly, in so far as you did this to one of the least of these brothers of mine, you did it to me" (Matt 25:35–40).

Sometimes, Colleen, we can become so caught up in and overwhelmed by the problems in our world, our society, and our communities that we don't remember that our work is not about changing society—a world we cannot completely change. Rather, it's about touching the lives that touch mine in a way that makes a difference. The Dalai Lama has said that "compassion occurs only between equals."[5] For those who have compassion, woundedness is not a place of judgment but a place of genuine meeting.

C. On Being Kind

For many people, life is difficult. On a daily basis, people struggle with all kinds of things—things that we would never know about. Sometimes they struggle with the most basic things—food, shelter, a job to support themselves and their families. At other times, it's more of a mental or emotional issue. For some, it might be a serious illness or disease. Situations and circumstances that we might never know about or experience are often extremely difficult for people. As the saying goes, we might not ever truly understand what goes on in the life of someone else, until we "walk in their shoes."

Being kind in life is so very important. Dag Hammarskjold in his book *Markings* said: "Goodness is something so simple, always to live for others, never to seek one's own advantage."[6] Being kind

---

5. Quoted from brainyquote.com/dalailama.html.

6. Hammarskjold, *Markings,* 87.

can be a basic stance in your life, Colleen, that helps others in a variety of ways and affects the kind of person you become. Often, you will never know the impact on a person's life when you are kind to them. Sometimes, it might be a kind word; sometimes, it might be something that you do for someone. No matter what it is, being kind to others brings healing and hope to people. A kind word can give people who are hurting a feeling that someone cares about them. A kind deed can give them a sense of hope—that you are willing to help them with their difficulties.

When you make kindness a basic stance in your life, Colleen, you can find so many opportunities each day to speak kindly to other people—those in your family, people you work with each day, a stranger on the street, a cashier at a store, your friends and neighbors. You can bring healing to people when you are kind to them.

At the same time, being kind to others also does something to yourself. It helps to build your own character because every time you are kind to another person in word or deed, you are quietly shaping the person you want to become. Because if you are genuinely being kind to someone, you can't be selfish at that moment, as Hammarskjold said. You can't be thinking about yourself. You have to go out of yourself to be kind to others. And every time we are not thinking about ourselves, we are allowing the Lord to form and shape us into the person He wants us to become.

And so, as you go about each day being kind to others, Colleen, know that you are a source of healing, hope and peace.

D. Lessons About Loving: A Dog's Story (Part 1)

Fr. Joe Breightner writes articles in *The Catholic Review* newspaper about life and spirituality. Back on July 19, 2007, he wrote an article about how dogs can teach us important aspects about life. We also know this about our Sadie! He shared a true story about his sister-in-law.

As a veterinarian, she had been called to examine a ten year old Irish wolfhound named Belker. The dogs' owners, Ron, his wife, Lisa and their little boy, Shane, were all very attached to

Belker, and they were hoping for a miracle. She examined Belker and found he was dying of cancer. She told the family that she couldn't do anything more for Belker, and offered to perform the euthanasia procedure for their pet in their home.

As the arrangements were made, Ron and Lisa said that they thought it would be good for six year old Shane to observe the procedure. They felt as though Shane might learn something from the experience.

The next day, the veterinarian felt the familiar catch in her throat as Belker's family surrounded him. Shane seemed so calm, petting the old dog for the last time, that she wondered if he really understood what was going on. Within a few minutes, Belker slipped peacefully away.

Although Shane was very attached to Belker, he seemed to accept his transition without any difficulty or confusion. Ron, Lisa and Shane sat together after Belker's death, wondering aloud about the sad fact that animal lives are shorter than human lives. Shane, who had been listening quietly said, "I know why." Startled, everyone turned to him. What came out of his mouth next stunned everyone. Shane simply said, "people are born so that they can learn to live a good life—like loving everybody all the time, and being nice, right?" Then, he continued, "well dogs already know how to do that, so they don't have to stay as long."

A touching story, isn't it Colleen? Live simply, love generously, care deeply, speak kindly.

E. Lessons About Loving: A Dog's Story (Part 2)

We can not only learn lessons about life from a dog's death, but also from a dog's life. If a dog were your teacher, you would learn things like:

1. When loved ones come home, always run to greet them.

2. Never pass up an opportunity for a joy ride.

3. Allow the experience of fresh air and the wind in your face to be pure ecstasy.

4. Take naps.

5. Stretch before rising.

6. Run, romp and play daily.

7. Thrive on attention and let people touch you.

8. Avoid biting when a simple growl will do.

9. On hot days, drink lots of water and lie under a shady tree.

10. Delight in the simple joy of a long walk.

11. Eat with gusto and enthusiasm. Stop when you have had enough.

12. Be loyal. Never pretend to be what you're not.

13. If you want what lies buried, dig until you find it.

14. When someone is having a bad day, be silent, sit close by, and nuzzle them slowly.

15. Always be grateful for each new day and for the blessing of you. Enjoy every moment of every day.

F. Try to Be a Rainbow in Someone's Cloud

In over thirty years of counseling, Colleen, I have learned a great deal about woundedness and healing from the people who have shared their life with me. I have seen many of them emerge from their woundedness more compassionate and altruistic than before. Perhaps this is because their own struggles have forced them to face into their own vulnerability. It has also allowed them to identify with the vulnerability of others. As a result of this process, they have found healing in their own lives and want to become more of a healing presence in the life of others.

Many people do not know that they can be an important healing presence in the life of others. They don't know that they can strengthen or diminish the life around them. The way they live each day simply may not reflect back to them their power to influence the lives of others. But it is important to realize that we all have the power to heal others. We can heal those we hardly know and even those we do not know at all. Many of the people I have worked with over the years have been taken completely by surprise by this power.

Without realizing it, we can influence the lives of others in very simple ways. When Emily became ill many years ago, bulimia was not yet a household word. Filled with guilt at her uncontrollable behavior, she had been taken to specialist after specialist until a doctor was able to identify the problem as something more than teenage rebellion. She had been hospitalized for a year and this had saved her life. Slowly, she fought her way back from the edge, surrounded by concerned adults who could not understand why she was bringing this on herself. Emily did not understand it either.

As she described it to me: "I just felt so *alone*, I could not stop myself, and at the worst of it I was not sure that it was possible to survive this. I was very afraid. I remember thinking that somewhere there must be someone else who has this problem, someone who has been able to heal from it. If they could live, maybe I could too." At the time, Emily did not meet another person with bulimia, but after many years of difficulty, she had somehow found her own way through this illness and was able to recover. She could not really explain why.

A few years ago, she was reading her evening newspaper and came across an announcement for a meeting of a bulimia support group. Emily was a middle-aged woman now and had not suffered from the problem for many years, but the idea of a support group intrigued her, and so she decided to attend a meeting to see what it was like. It had been a powerful experience. The desperately ill young people there had touched her heart and while she felt unable to help them, she cared about them and continued going back. Other than saying she had bulimia as a girl she had not revealed a great deal more about herself but had simply sat and listened to the stories of others.

As she was about to leave one of these meetings, she was stopped by a painfully thin young girl who thanked her for coming and told her how much it had meant to know her. The girl's eyes had been filled with tears. Emily had responded with her usual graciousness, but she had been puzzled. She could not recall ever speaking to this girl and did not even know her name. As she drove home, she wondered how she could have forgotten something so important to someone else. She was almost home before she understood. Her husband, who met her at the front door, was surprised to see that she had been crying. "Emily, what is wrong?" he asked. "I have become the person I needed to meet, Harry," she told him as she walked into the house.

Sometimes, our presence, Colleen, shines through us, even when we are not aware of it. We become a healing presence to others simply by being who we are.

People have been healing each other in a variety of ways since the beginning of time. Long before there were doctors and therapists, we were there for each other. The healing of our present woundedness in life may lie in recognizing and reclaiming the capacity we all have to heal each other. We need to understand and use the enormous power we possess in the simplest of human relationships: the strength of a touch, the blessing of forgiveness, the grace of someone else taking you just as you are and finding in you an unsuspected goodness.

Everyone has been wounded in life. It is the wisdom gained from our wounds and from our own experiences of suffering that makes us able to heal. Becoming an expert is less important than remembering and trusting the wholeness in myself and everyone else. Expertise might cure, but wounded people can best be healed by other wounded people. Only other wounded people can understand what is needed, because the healing of suffering is compassion, not expertise.

G. On Becoming a Good Listener

Some years ago, I attended a day long continuing education course presented by Carl Rogers, a pioneering humanistic psychotherapist. Rogers approach to therapy, called unconditional positive regard, was very popular at the time.

Rogers was a deeply intuitive man, and as he spoke to us about how he worked with his patients, he often paused to put into words what he did instinctively and naturally. After explaining his approach to his clients, Rogers offered us a demonstration. One of the participants from the audience volunteered to act as his client and they rearranged their chairs to sit opposite one another. As Rogers turned toward him and was about to begin the demonstration session, he stopped and looked thoughtfully at the audience. Then he went on to speak. "Before every session, I take a moment to remember my humanity," he said. "There is no experience that this man has that I cannot share with him, no fear that I cannot understand, no suffering that I cannot care about, because I too am human. No matter how deep his wound, he does not need to be ashamed in front of me. I too am vulnerable. And because of this, 'I am enough.' Whatever his story, he no longer needs to be alone with it. This is what will allow his healing to begin."

The session that followed was profound. Rogers conducted it without saying a single word, conveying to his client simply by the quality of his attention a total acceptance of him exactly as he was. The participant began to talk and the session rapidly became a great deal more than the demonstration of a technique. In the safe presence of Rogers' total acceptance, he began to shed his masks, hesitantly at first and then more and more easily. As each mask fell, Rogers welcomed the one behind it unconditionally, until finally we glimpsed the struggle and the beauty of this person's life. It was truly amazing to see how this kind of profound listening, total acceptance and being received in such a complete way could allow a person to become vulnerable and begin the journey toward healing.

What Rogers was pointing out Colleen, is a very wise and basic principle of a healing relationship. Whatever the expertise we have acquired, the greatest gift we bring to anyone who is suffering is our humanness.

Listening is the oldest and perhaps the most powerful tool of healing. It is often through the quality of our listening and not the wisdom of our words that we are able to effect the most profound changes in the people around us. When we truly listen, we offer an opportunity for healing. Our listening creates a safe place—a sanctuary—within a person to explore those parts of ourselves that have been hurt or wounded by our life experiences. It is because of our listening and acceptance, that others find healing.

I suspect that the most basic and powerful way to connect with another person is to listen. Just listen. This is what Carl Rogers understood in a very profound way. Perhaps the most important thing we ever give each other is our attention. And especially if it is given from the heart. When people are talking, there is no need to do anything but receive them. Just take them in. Listen to what they are saying. Care about it. Most of the time, caring about it is even more important than understanding it. Most of us don't value ourselves or our love enough to know this. It has taken me a long time to believe in the power of simply listening, and saying "I'm so sorry," when someone is in pain, and sincerely meaning it.

One of my clients once told me that when she tried to tell her story, people often interrupted to tell her that they once had something just like that happen to them. Subtly, her pain became a story about themselves. Eventually, she stopped talking to most people. It was just too lonely. We connect through listening. When we interrupt what someone is saying to let them know that we understand, we move the focus of attention to ourselves. When we listen, they know we care. Many people who are hurting talk about the relief they feel when someone just listens to them.

In my own counseling practice, Colleen, I have even learned to respond to someone crying by just listening. In my earlier years as a therapist, I used to reach for the tissues, until I realized that passing a person a tissue may be just another way to shut them down, to take them out of their experience of sadness and grief. Now, I just listen. When they have cried all they need to cry, they find me there with them.

Most people like to talk, Colleen. Becoming a good listener takes practice. It can be difficult at times. But if you stick with it, you will find that listening creates a holy silence. When you listen generously to people, they can hear the truth in themselves, often for the first time. And in the silence of listening, you bring healing to the other person. A loving silence often has far more power to heal and to connect than the most well intentioned words.

H. The Holy Shadow

Years ago, I read a novel by Graham Greene, entitled *The Honorary Consul*. In one of the scenes in this book, several people were sitting around a table after dinner discussing what was important to them in life. One of the characters made an observation that I have never forgotten—even after all these years. "Caring is the only really dangerous thing in life."[7]

Over the years, I have come to understand the importance of this statement, Colleen. It is so true. Why? Because in order to truly care for another person, you have to become vulnerable. In order to truly care for someone, you have to forget about yourself and be open to others. Both of these ideas—becoming vulnerable and forgetting about ourselves are not very popular concepts in our society. Rather than wanting to become vulnerable which can lead to being hurt, we try to protect ourselves. Rather than wanting to forget about ourselves, we are encouraged in our society to always strive to put ourselves forward—to become number one.

Another reason it's difficult to care for others is because many of us live such a fast paced life that we don't have time to give to others. When you are constantly in motion, it is difficult to really "see" others. It's easy to simply pass them by. A fourth reason why it is challenging to be a caring person is because of our own daily struggles. Our own schedules, time commitments, busyness, fears, anxieties and worries get in the way of our efforts to care for others.

We know that Jesus was truly a caring person in so many ways. Whether he was healing, curing, forgiving, touching, praying, spending time with others, going out of his way to visit someone, and ultimately dying for us, he was willing to forget about himself so he could genuinely care for others.

7. Greene, *The Honorary Consul*, front book cover.

However, it's also important to realize that we might care for others in life far more than we realize. Many simple, ordinary things that we do each day can affect those around us in some very profound ways: the unexpected phone call, a brief touch, a quick email, sending a card to someone, the willingness to listen generously, the warm smile of recognition, or by being kind to someone. We can even care for total strangers and be cared for by them. Sometimes, big messages can come in small packages.

I think what is really important for us to understand, Colleen, is that becoming more of a caring person requires us to develop a basic "stance" in life, so to speak, in which we want to care for others. Then, as opportunities arise each day, we can act upon them.

There are many ways to care for and strengthen the lives of people around us. Often, it will involve doing something for someone. Sometimes, these opportunities come to us in the most unexpected ways.

Joan was a librarian who would soon be forty. She had always lived alone. Charitably speaking, Joan could be described as very, very plain. However, her sisters and her mother were truly beautiful women. When you looked at Joan, you could tell her clothes were not very becoming to her. She wore no jewelry or make-up and her hair was pulled back with a rubber band into a ponytail. Her finest feature was her eyes. Clear and gray, they were now filled with tears.

Life is not easy for a plain woman. From early childhood, she had felt ashamed of her looks and was painfully shy. The response of others to her simply confirmed her sense of wrongness. In school, children made fun of her appearance. As a teenager, her peers had avoided her. Her family, while loyal, were often apologetic about the way she looked. Many years before, she had simply given up. In her entire life, she had never had an intimate relationship. She felt at ease only in her home or in the library. "Librarians are invisible," she told me. She spent her days at work and her evenings in front of the TV. She had lived this way for a long time.

As her fortieth birthday grew closer, Joan became more depressed. I worried about her and began to see her more often. I tried to offer her a place of acceptance and caring, but in the end it was not me, but my clients, who healed her.

As she sat in my waiting room, week after week, she began to respond to the others she saw there. Many of them were hurting like she was. She had never met people like them before, and she was surprised that she felt so comfortable with them. Although she was shy, she eventually began to speak with some of them. She had also noticed that other people often came with these clients, people who drove or shopped or helped in a variety of ways. They were genuinely caring people. After thinking about this for a while, she hesitantly told me that if some of my clients had no one or if their families needed an extra hand, she would be glad to help.

This was how Joan met Bill. He was a handsome thirty-two year old man who had become HIV positive about a year after his partner was diagnosed with AIDS. Bill had nursed him through his long, progressive illness and ultimate death. Slowly, he too became sick and needed help.

At first, Joan drove Bill to doctors' appointments much as she drove several others. However, most of the others had some family, but Bill was alone. As time went on, she began to shop for him and then to cook extra food at home, freeze it, and take it to him for dinner. They became friends. As things became worse, his parents had flown in to see him several times. They were older now and it had been difficult for them at first, but they were a close family and had been able to support Bill in ways that really mattered. Joan had met them too, and liked them. Like Bill, they were kind people.

Within a year, Bill became very ill. His parents had wanted him to come home but he had lived in California for many years and wanted to stay there. He had applied for hospice care but discovered he was not eligible because there was no one living with him who could act as his caregiver. Many of his closest friends had already died and he had no one to turn to for help. After much prayer and reflection, Joan moved in.

Bill died in the spring. When I heard the news I called Joan because I was concerned about her and wondered if she would be able to handle things. Her depression had lifted somewhat over the past several months, but I knew Bill's death would be a great blow to her.

A few weeks later, she came to see me and told me she had been visiting Bill's parents and had attended his funeral. As she talked about the events that had led to his death, I noticed that she was wearing lipstick. When I commented on this, she looked away from me and seemed to blush. Continuing with her story, she told me about something that had happened shortly before Bill died. He had been very weak and mostly bedridden for some time. One morning, he had not been doing well, and so she called him from the library several times during the day. The hospice social worker and the nurse visited him daily and often a neighbor would look in, but as the day went on she worried about his being at home alone until she finished work.

Coming home, she had run up the stairs, her arms full of groceries. She opened the door, calling his name loudly so that he could hear her in his bedroom. But Bill was not in his bedroom. Fully dressed in a jacket, shirt, and tie, he was sitting in the living room waiting for her. His clothes, still elegant, looked as if they had been bought for a much larger man, but his hair was carefully combed and he had shaved. The effort involved was hard for her to even imagine.

Stunned, she asked him why he had gotten dressed. He had looked at her for a moment. Then, he eased off the couch, and, getting down on one knee, he had asked her to marry him. She had put the groceries down then and helped him up. Hugging him for the first time, she told him how very important he was to her.

I looked at her in silence. Still blushing, she met my eye. "In my heart I did marry him you know," she told me. "He will be here with me always." Sometimes, the deepest healing comes from the natural fit between two wounded people's lives. If we have this basic stance of wanting to care for others in life, Colleen, we will discover there are opportunities even when we don't know it at the time.

There is a Sufi story about a man who was so good that the angels ask God to give him the gift of miracles. God wisely tells them to ask him if that is what he would wish. So the angels visit this good man and offer him first the gift of healing by hands, then the gift of conversion of souls, and lastly the gift of virtue. He refuses them all. They insist that he choose a gift or they will choose one for him. "Very well," he replies. "I ask that I may do a great deal of good without ever knowing it." The angels were perplexed. They took counsel and resolved upon the following plan: every time this holy man's shadow fell behind him, it would have the power to cure disease, soothe pain, and comfort sorrow. As he walked, behind him his shadow made arid paths green, caused withered plants to bloom, gave water to dried up streams, fresh color to pale children, and joy to unhappy men and women. He simply went about his daily life diffusing virtue as the stars diffuse light and the flowers scent, without ever being aware of it. The people, respecting his humility, followed him silently, never speaking to him about his miracles. Soon, they even forgot his name and simply called him "the holy shadow." It is comforting to think that we may care for others in ways that we don't even realize.

In a similar way, Colleen, always remember that we can care for others simply by our presence. We don't necessarily "do" anything for someone. It's just our presence that makes all the difference and brings healing and comfort into their lives. This is so important to realize because sometimes in difficult or tragic situations, there is nothing we can really do to alleviate the pain. But our presence can make all the difference

I. Buy a Plant

There is a plant in my office. It sits in one corner of the room. Over the years, it has become a conversation piece for many of my clients. They would often ask how it was doing. Was it thriving? How was it growing? Did it take much time to care for it?

Every client comes to counseling because in some way they live in a psychological environment that makes growth difficult. Emotionally speaking, they are trying to find a way to grow and thrive like my plant. Sarah was a remarkable woman who was referred to me because of depression and anxiety. The owner of a successful interior design firm, she was on friendly terms with many very creative people. Yet she had come because of a deep loneliness and a long string of self-destructive behaviors and relationships with men. She was a large woman of great warmth and humor and had a wonderful laugh.

Born in Ireland of a socially prominent Catholic family, she was raised in a traditional home in which she had felt safe and protected. As a young girl, she attended Catholic schools and traveled with her family to many wonderful places. It had been a pleasant and comfortable life.

"When did all that change?" I asked her. Painfully, she told me about an evening when she had left her boarding school on an errand and had been raped at knife point. She had received very little honest support from her overwhelmed parents or her church, who dealt with her shame by covering over it with silence. Shortly afterwards, she had left Ireland and moved to the States to live with an aunt.

Although this happened twenty-five years ago, the rape had left her deeply wounded, vulnerable and shamed. She became unable to set personal boundaries or take control of her life. She took whatever came her way and tried to make the most of it. She didn't really believe that she could change things. However, at work, she was powerful and very competent, making shrewd decisions and running a successful business in a highly competitive field.

For more than a year, we talked about her experience which opened many old wounds and allowed some healing to begin. It also allowed us to explore some conclusions she had drawn about herself and about life. After some months of this, we began to examine how she lived her own life. For many years, she had spent her life without knowing how to grow emotionally or how to work through all these feelings. I told her that she had very little experience in knowing how to care for herself and I suggested she begin a practice to enable her to learn this. "Did I mean meditation?" she asked. "Not exactly," I said. "Buy a plant." She laughed and said she did not think that she could keep a plant alive. But that was just the point. Although she was doubtful, she agreed to try.

Over the next several months, Sarah struggled to keep the plant alive. Her task was to pay attention to it every day, noticing its needs and responding to them. At first it was touch and go. Her plant suffered from overindulgence followed by periods of neglect, much like Sarah herself. "Listen, more carefully," I encouraged her. "If you really pay attention, it will show you what it needs."

Sarah's plant was tenacious. Despite some hard times, it would recover and continue to grow. Sarah began to admire its resilience and she began to see something of herself in it. She spoke to me about its strength and ability to continue to grow despite some difficulties. Gradually, she got better at recognizing its needs.

At about this time, Sarah began to consider making some changes in her life. The demands of her work were enormous, and she had very little time for herself. Building on a new trust in her own judgment and her ability to know what she needed, she sold her business and opened a design school. Then, she met a good, kind man and began dating him. Over the next several months, as she moved into this new life and this relationship, she no longer felt a need for our sessions.

A few years later, I received an invitation to her wedding. She and her husband are now settled in Virginia in their first home. Proudly, she showed me pictures. Her yard was enormous. When I commented on its beauty, she smiled, "I planted it myself."

As a therapist yourself, Colleen, it is interesting to know that Carl Jung sometimes worked with his patients by asking them where they had been just before they came to his office. Often, they had been caught up in the most mundane and ordinary activities like going to the grocery store, driving a car or visiting a friend. By carefully listening to the way in which they had done these things, asking thoughtful questions and uncovering automatic and habitual responses, Jung would clarify a person's entire way of living, their strengths and their limitations.

I have come to suspect that each person's subjective world is probably the pattern of our most fundamental beliefs which is reflected in the smallest of our choices and behaviors. For example, the way in which we go to the grocery store may tell us everything about the way in which we live our lives. The way we tend to care for a plant may be the way we tend to take care of ourselves. Healing requires a certain willingness to hear and respond to life's needs. Sarah had never listened to her needs. In fact, she did not know how to listen to them. Because of this, she did not know how to take care of herself emotionally and psychologically. My plant was a better teacher of this sort of thing than I was. Sometimes, the most unexpected things can become like a co-therapist.

So, in order for us to care for others, Colleen, we first need to learn how to take care of ourselves. I am reminded of the announcement that a flight attendant gives to the passengers in an airplane right before takeoff. "If the cabin loses pressure, the oxygen masks will fall from above. Put on your own mask first before you try to help the person next to you." We need to care for ourselves first so that we don't burn out and then we can allow our caring to overflow to others.

J. "We're All Just Walking Each Other Home" Rumi

Perhaps for many of us, what is more difficult than caring for others or caring for ourselves, Colleen, is our struggle to allow others to care for us. As the character in Graham Greene's novel said: "caring is the only really dangerous thing in life." It becomes dangerous because when we allow ourselves to be cared for, we allow ourselves to be vulnerable. And in our society, we are taught to be autonomous, strong and independent. When we allow ourselves to become vulnerable, we open ourselves to being hurt. Doing this can require a great deal of courage. We simply are not used to having people care for us.

In Mitch Albom's book, *Tuesday with Morrie,* TV personality Ted Koppel asked Morrie about how he faced the end of life. "Ted," he said, "when all this started, I asked myself, 'Am I going to withdraw from the world, like most people do, or am I going to live?' I decided I'm going to live—or at least try to live—the way I want, with dignity, with courage, with humor, with composure. There are some mornings when I cry and cry and mourn for myself. Some mornings, I'm so angry and bitter. But it doesn't last too long. Then I get up and say, 'I want to live'. . . . So far I've been able to do it. Will I be able to continue? I don't know. But I'm betting on myself that I will."[8]

The two men continued to speak about death and the afterlife. They spoke about Morrie's increasing dependency on other people. He already needed help eating and sitting and moving from place to place. Then, Koppel asked Morrie about what he dreaded most about his slow, insidious decay? Morrie paused for a moment and then told Koppel, "well, Ted, one day soon, someone's gonna have to wipe my ass."[9]

Asking for help, receiving care from someone else when we need it is extremely difficult for many of us. In our society, it is often seen as a sign of weakness. We are supposed to be strong. We are supposed to take care of ourselves. In my counseling practice, I saw these beliefs lived out in the lives of so many people—especially men. Our culture teaches men to believe in so many ways that it is unmanly to ask for help and that you are weak if you say you have needs. And so, men often will not share their weakness with anyone. However, they often pay the price for this in their own personal lives and relationships.

Allowing ourselves to receive care from others makes us vulnerable. And maybe for some of us, this is another reason why this whole notion of caring can be seen as dangerous. Many people fear being vulnerable because this can open us up to being hurt and people try to protect themselves from being hurt at all costs. However, at the heart of any real intimacy is a certain vulnerability. It is difficult to trust someone with your vulnerability unless you know that they truly care for you and that you will not be judged. Rather than protecting ourselves from being hurt, it is really our imperfections and even our pain that can draw others close to us.

8. Albom, *Tuesdays with Morrie*, 21–22.
9. Ibid., 22.

Later on, in *Tuesdays with Morrie,* Morrie was reflecting on how difficult it was to be dependent on someone else. He said it took him time to get used to this because, in a way, it was complete surrender to the disease. By now, the most personal and basic things had been taken from him—dressing himself, going to the bathroom, blowing his nose. With the exception of breathing and swallowing his food, he was dependent on others for nearly everything.

Mitch asked Morrie how he managed to be vulnerable and to stay positive through this struggle.

> 'Mitch, it's funny,' he said. 'I'm an independent person, so my inclination was to fight all of this—being helped from the car, having someone else dress me. I felt a little ashamed, because our culture tells us we should be ashamed if we can't wipe our own behind. But then I figured, forget what the culture says. I have ignored the culture much of my life. I am not going to be ashamed. What's the big deal?'
>
> 'And you know what? The strangest thing.'
>
> 'What's that?'
>
> 'I began to *enjoy* my dependency. Now I enjoy it when they turn me over on my side and rub cream on my behind so I don't get sores. Or, when they wipe my brow, or they massage my legs, I revel in it. I close my eyes and soak it up. And it seems very familiar to me.
>
> It's like going back to being a child again. Someone to bathe you. Someone to lift you. We all know how to be a child. It's inside all of us. For me, it's just remembering how to enjoy it.
>
> The truth is, when our mothers held us, rocked us, stroked our heads—none of us ever got enough of that. We all yearn in some way to return to those days when we were completely taken care of—unconditional love, unconditional attention. Most of us didn't get enough. I know I didn't.'[10]

Continuing to reflect on what he had learned from this disease, Morrie said, "the most important thing in life is to learn how

10. Ibid., 115–16.

to give out love, and let it come in." His voice dropped to a whisper. "Let it come in. We think we don't deserve love, we think if we let it in we'll become too soft. But a wise man named Levine said it right. He said. 'love is the only rational act.'"

He repeated it carefully, pausing for effect. "Love is the only rational act."[11]

Morrie had learned that his vulnerability was not dangerous as the character in Green's novel suggested. For him, it had become a strength. His dependency on others was not a weakness but something that allowed him to connect with others on a deeper level. His ability to eventually allow himself to receive the care of others gave him the ability to experience how much he loved others and how much they loved him. In the end, he understood that "love is the only rational act."

K. Clothe Others with Respect

Through the years, Dorothy Day has been a model as a person who loved, lived with, and dedicated her life to serving the poor. She is the co-founder of the Catholic Worker Movement which still continues today.

Psychiatrist, teacher, and author Robert Coles has written a moving account of the day in 1952 when, as a young and discouraged medical student, he met Dorothy. He found himself one afternoon at the Catholic Worker soup kitchen, having made an earlier decision to engage in some useful volunteer work. This is the story of his first encounter with Dorothy.

> She was sitting at a table, talking with a woman who was, I quickly realized, quite drunk, yet determined to carry on a conversation. . . . The woman to whom Dorothy Day was talking . . . had a large purple birthmark along the right side of her forehead. She kept touching it as she uttered one exclamatory remark after another, none of which seemed to get the slightest rise from the person sitting opposite her.

11. Ibid., 52.

I found myself increasingly confused by what seemed to be an interminable essentially absurd exchange taking place between two middle-aged women. When would it end—the alcoholic ranting and the silent nodding, occasionally interrupted by a brief question, which only served, maddeningly, to wind up the already over-talkative one rather than wind her down? Finally, silence fell upon the room. She got up and came over to me. She said, 'Are you waiting to talk to one of us?'

One of us: with those three words she had cut through layers of self-importance, a life-time of bourgeois privilege, and scraped the hard bone of pride. . . . With those three words, she had indirectly told me what the Catholic Worker Movement is all about and what she herself was like.[12]

During the years he knew her, Coles would learn many things from Dorothy Day, but this particular lesson would serve as a basis for everything else. Dorothy's use of the words "one of us" placed the ranting, alcoholic woman on a par with herself, and, for that moment at least, clothed her with respect. That afternoon in the Catholic Worker house, Dorothy and her companion were, to use a phrase by psychiatrist Gerald May, two notes in the human symphony—one harmonious and one discordant, one sweet and one harsh, but both part of the same song. Dorothy was possessed by a connection of the presence of Christ in everyone. It was this certainty of his radiant love alive in every person that compelled her to live in service of that love, regardless of how unlikely or unattractive a vessel she might find it.

We seem to live in an age today, Colleen, when this idea of reverence and respect has lost much of its importance in life. When we look around us, there seems to be so much irreverence and disrespect. The way we often treat one another is an indication of that. But it is such an important dimension of life. It colors so much of how we go about living each day.

12. Coles, *Dorothy Day,* xviii.

So, what does it mean to be reverent and respectful? While this is certainly not an exhaustive list, I would say it means some of the following things.

I think it has a lot to do with the way Dorothy treated that lady who was drunk. She was able to look beyond her drinking problem and saw her being a child of God and possessing the presence of Christ. Then, because of this, she was willing to spend time with her and in the process gave her dignity. Having reverence and respect for others, enables us to have a basic stance in life where we see the presence of Christ in everyone. This, then, will allow us to treat each person with dignity and respect.

Secondly, I think having reverence and respect means basically trying to live the Golden Rule which encourages us to always treat others as we would like to be treated. This will encourage us to never look down on anyone, never think yourself better than anyone because very often, we don't know their story.

Thirdly, having reverence and respect for others means that we don't use people for our own pleasure or gain. We don't use people to get ahead in life or to gain something for ourselves. With this kind of outlook, we can choose to treat others with kindness and compassion.

Finally, Colleen, I think being reverent and respectful also gives us a way of treating all of life, i.e. our planet, mother nature, animals etc. This vision allows us to realize that we are not here to dominate anyone or anything but rather to do our part to share and preserve all of life for future generations. When we see life in this way, we can do our part to make it a more gentle world.

L. Live Your Life so as to Make a Difference

Sometimes, we can feel very unimportant in life, Colleen, and believe that what we do with our lives is not very meaningful. But this is simply not the case. Some years ago, one of my clients shared an early struggle with me. When she was younger, she said that it had taken her a long time to realize that she had an impact on the people around her. For years, she suffered from shyness and

WALKING EACH OTHER HOME

a lack of self-esteem. She felt as though she was invisible to others and that her presence or absence had little or no influence on anyone. As a young adult, she would often not respond to a written invitation or return a phone message. Sometimes, she would leave a party without a word to anyone, including the host or hostess. It simply never occurred to her that anyone might notice that she had not responded or that she was no longer there. Years later, she was stunned to discover that all those years she had been seen as aloof and rude and that her behavior often hurt people. She certainly had never meant to do that. However, she felt so badly about herself, she truly believed that her presence didn't matter.

Many people are like this client, Colleen. They don't believe that they make a difference in life. But it is so important to believe in yourself and to know that your presence always makes a difference. Sir Thomas Browne wrote: "we carry within us the wonders we seek without us."[13] We all have the power to affect others, probably more than we realize. Believing in yourself allows you to live each day believing that you can always make a difference.

There is a story about a starfish that emphasizes this idea. It seems as though there was an elderly man who used to walk along a beach at low tide, picking up starfish drying in the sun and gently throwing them back into the ocean. He had been doing this for some time when a jogger overtook him and asked him what he was doing. The old man explained that the starfish would die in the sun, and so he was throwing them back into the ocean. Astounded, the younger man began to laugh. "Why, old fellow, don't waste your time. Can't you see that there are hundreds and hundreds of starfish on this beach? And thousands of beaches in this world? And another low tide tomorrow? What makes you think that you can make a difference?" Still laughing, he ran on down the beach.

The old man watched him for a long time. Then he walked on and before long he passed another starfish. Stooping, he picked it up and looked at it thoughtfully. Then, gently, he threw it back into the ocean. "Made a difference to that one," he said to himself.

---

13. Quoted from brainyquote.com/sirthomasbrowne.html.

So much of life involves touching the lives that touch yours in a way that makes a difference. Believing in yourself allows this to happen continually. Mary had studied and practiced medicine for more than twenty five years, rising to the top of her specialty, first as a pediatrician, then as a neonatologist, and finally as an expert in the care of premature infants. Unmarried, she had dedicated her life to the survival of the infants and she had been recognized as one of the country's best authorities in this demanding and highly technical speciality.

When she came to see me, she was angry and depressed. As we talked over the next several months, she explained that more and more of her time was spent defending the needs of her tiny patients for care. She spoke of the hours she now had to spend every day on the phone, the endless amount of paper work, the total frustration of arguing with insurance company employees, day after day, justifying the value of a premature baby's life in terms of the cost of needed care.

"I just can't do it anymore," she said. Mary had seemed to be at the end of her rope. Together, we explored other options for her in terms of changing careers. Just giving her the freedom to talk and look at other possibilities seemed to help. Gradually, her depression lifted and slowly she began to feel better.

One day, Mary called and asked to see me. With tears in her eyes, she told me that somehow she had forgotten that every phone call, every letter, every form that she fills out matters. "I was so caught up in the insanities of the system that I didn't remember that my work is not about changing a world I cannot change. It's about touching the lives that touch mine in a way that makes a difference. I used to do this in one way; now I do it in another."

In the final analysis, Colleen, no matter how great or how small the need, we can only bless one life at a time. Believe in yourself and know that your presence matters when you think about visiting someone who might be sick, lonely or in the hospital. When you send a card or an email to someone who might be hurting, you make a difference. When you become involved in some issue, cause or idea that you feel passionate about, your presence matters. When you take the time to be present with and talk with someone who needs to talk, believe that you are truly helping.

There are so many ways to make a difference in life, Colleen. Never sell yourself short.

M. "You Have Seen Me and I Am Grateful"

As you know, Colleen, I have been in the counseling profession for over thirty years. It has been an excellent career choice for me and one that I have thoroughly enjoyed. Now, you are in the same profession and although it is still fairly new for you, it seems to be a very good choice for you too and one which you are also enjoying.

Over the years, I have thought about my career in terms of what it has meant to me. Now that I am retired, I have had the chance to think more about this and would like to share some of my ideas with you. I would like to do this, not because you will necessarily view your career in the same way that I have, but only to give you my perspective, especially since we are in the same career.

People come to counseling for many reasons. Some come looking for advice or to sort out a problem. Others come looking for a safe environment where they can share something they have never told anyone before. Still others come to find comfort from the storms of life while others look for help in grieving the loss of a loved one. Looking for help with a problematic relationship or trying to sort out family issues as well as career issues can also be a major reason for seeking help. No matter what the issue is, people are always looking for a safe place where they know they will be accepted in a non-judgmental way.

I think one of the reasons this profession has always been so appealing to me is because of my desire to help people. For some reason, this has always been a major part of my personality and I have found in my career as a psychotherapist a certain kind of fulfillment. However, I must also admit that I wanted to earn a good living in order to help support our family. Fortunately, I have had the opportunity to satisfy both of these desires through my career in counseling.

Over the years, I have come to understand that there have been several stages in how I have viewed my profession. In the beginning, when I was in graduate school, I remember studying very diligently because I wanted to learn how to be a good therapist. Although it might sound simplistic, Colleen, I truly wanted to help people and become the best possible therapist I could be. In class, I learned many counseling theories and had the opportunity to practice them during my internships. I would meet a client, listen to them, establish rapport, diagnose them, decide what counseling strategy would be most beneficial, and go to work. I was putting my knowledge to work. The model I was taught focused on what I as a therapist had learned about this particular problem the person was experiencing, and supposedly gave me the tools, the strategies to help them. I was implementing my knowledge. But I was very young then and didn't have much life experience. Maybe more importantly, I didn't have much wisdom then either. However, during this time, Andrew died and my struggle through the years of trying to make sense of that reality, began a process in me of gaining some wisdom and understanding that helping people in life is much more than simply having knowledge. The wisdom we gain from our life experiences are also important. My experience of losing Andrew enabled me to gradually understand so many things about loss, sorrow, life, and healing. It has greatly affected my understanding of my career as a psychotherapist.

During these early years, I think I spent a lot of time learning how to fix life, only to discover at the end of the day that life is not broken. It is a mystery to be lived. As the writer Rainer Maria Rilke says, "be patient toward all that is unsolved in your heart, and try to love the questions themselves."[14] Although this approach to counseling and to life in general is challenging, it is also more freeing. As a therapist, I have found that realizing we don't have to fix everyone and every situation gives us more opportunities to reflect on the important questions life has to offer and to realize that often there are no easy or simple answers to many of these questions.

14. Rilke, *Letters to a Young Poet*, 35.

I have also discovered as a therapist, Colleen, that I don't know what is needed much of the time and really, even more surprising, I don't need to know. But I have also learned that if I listen attentively to someone, to their essential self—their soul, as it were—I often find that, at their deepest level, they can sense the direction of their own healing. If I can remain open to that, without expectations of what someone is "supposed to do," or how they are supposed to change in order to "get better," what can happen is amazing. For me, this approach is much wiser and healthier than any way of fixing their situation or easing their pain and sorrow that I might devise on my own.

So, I no longer have many theories about people. I don't simply diagnose them or decide what their problem is. I don't even believe that I have to fix them. I simply meet with them and listen. As we sit together, I don't even have an agenda, but I know that something will emerge from our conversation over time that is a part of a larger coherent pattern that neither of us can fully see at this moment. So I sit with them, listen, and wait.

The Celestine Prophecy offers a simple and helpful description of the possibility within all human relationships. It says that there is a way of relating to others that encourages a person to deliberately listen to the hidden beauty in themselves. The place of their beauty is often the place of their greatest integrity. When you listen, the integrity and wholeness in others moves closer together. Your presence and attention strengthens and helps them to hear it in themselves. It has been my experience, Colleen, that presence and listening is a more powerful catalyst for change than analysis, and that we can know beyond doubt things we can never understand.

As a psychotherapist, I have had the privilege of accompanying people on their journeys of discovery. In some way, this journey always involves striving for wholeness. It has been my experience that counseling can be very helpful to discover this wholeness. But first, people need the opportunity to identify the problems and barriers that keep them from growing. This is part of the process of striving for wholeness. So many people are wounded in many different ways. Spiritual writer Henri Nouwen says that we are all wounded people and this allows us to become wounded healers. I think you will find through the years, Colleen, that facing your own wounds in life will make you a better therapist.

Through the years, I have been fortunate to accompany many people as they have discovered in themselves an unexpected strength, a courage beyond what they would have thought possible, an unexpected sense of compassion or a capacity for love deeper than they had ever dreamed. I have watched people abandon values that they have never questioned before and find the courage to live in new ways.

For people striving for wholeness, perhaps the image of an acorn can be helpful. What you can see and touch about an acorn—its color, its weight, and its hardness—will never hint at the secret of its potential. This secret is not directly measurable, but given the proper conditions over time, it will become visible.

Within an acorn, there is something waiting to unfold that will become an oak tree. An acorn is defined by this capacity. Something can be the size, shape, weight, texture, and color of an acorn, but without this hidden power to become an oak tree, it is not an acorn. In the same way, our essential humanity is always striving for growth and wholeness.

Every acorn yearns toward the full expression of its nature and uses every opportunity to realize its capacity to become an oak tree. Similarly, there is a natural yearning toward wholeness in all of us. Counseling gives people the opportunity to strive for this wholeness in their own lives. Sometimes, their wholeness is buried by personality issues or problems of one kind or another. Working with people on this journey of discovery can be very rewarding.

Another way I have come to understand my counseling practice, Colleen, is to understand that my office is a place of refuge. It is not a gentle world. People struggle with the storms of life in a variety of ways. Often, the way they try to cope doesn't allow them to grow. But I have always felt that if I could provide a safe environment in my office where each person could be accepted in a safe and non-judgmental way, they could find a way of sorting out their issues and become more peaceful.

I read a story one time about Sarah, a highly skilled AIDS doctor, who kept a picture of her grandmother in her home and sat in front of it for a few minutes every day before she left for work. Her grandmother was an Italian-born woman who held her family very close. She was also a very wise woman. Once, when Sarah was very small, her kitten was killed in an accident. It was her first experience of death and she was devastated. Her parents had encouraged her not to be sad, telling her that her kitten was in heaven now with God. Despite these assurances, she had not been comforted. She had prayed to God, asking Him to give her kitten back. But God did not respond.

In her sorrow, she turned to her grandmother and asked "why?" Her grandmother had not told her that her kitten was in heaven like so many other adults had done. Instead, she had simply held her and reminded her of the time when her grandfather had died. She, too, had prayed to God, but God had not brought grandpa back. She did not know why. Sarah laid her head on her grandmother's shoulder and sobbed. When she was finally able to look up, she saw her grandmother was crying as well.

Although her grandmother could not answer her questions, a great sadness had been lifted and she felt able to go on. All the assurances that Peaches was in heaven had not given her strength or peace. "My grandmother was a lap," Sarah said, "a place of refuge." This doctor knew a great deal about AIDS, but what she really wanted to be for her patients was a lap. A place from which they could face what they had to face and not be alone.

Finding refuge does not mean hiding from life, Colleen. It means finding a place of strength, the capacity to live the life we have been given with greater courage. This is what I have come to believe about my counseling room. It's a place of refuge, a lap for people to rest in—in order for them to sort out their issues and find the strength to continue their journeys in a positive way. It's a place where people can share with you things they may have never spoken about, where they can find some healing from their wounds in life. Maybe what everyone needs is a lap.

I also think you will find, Colleen, that your success as a counselor will be based on trust. The more your clients trust you, the more you will be able to help them. This bond of trust will allow you to say some difficult things to your clients at times and they will be able to listen to you because they trust you. They know you are there only to try and help them.

It is also important to remember, Colleen, that in your work as a counselor, you will not be able to help everyone who comes to you. For a variety of reasons, some people will not continue to come to their sessions, some will not take your advice and others will not be able to sustain their efforts to change some dimension of their lives. In my early years as a therapist, this was difficult for me to accept. I remember thinking at times that I had failed in some way, that I should have been able to help them. It was only with time and more experience that I realized that this was ok and that hopefully, these clients would find other people or other ways of finding the help they needed in order to continue to grow.

Another reflection about my career as a psychotherapist, Colleen, is to remember that sometimes you will not be able to know at any given moment how much you have helped someone. Sometimes, counseling someone is like the seed that is planted which will bear fruit later on. Rachel was a young teenager in high school that I began to work with because of some behavioral issues. At one point in one of our sessions, she told me that she wanted to become a police officer. But she doubted that she would ever be able to accomplish this. For all kinds of reasons, she doubted herself. However, during the years that we worked together, she really did work on her issues. Gradually, she made enough progress that enabled us to end our sessions. For several years, she stayed in touch with an occasional phone call or card to let me know how she was doing. Then one day, about ten months ago, I received a call from her telling me that she was now a police woman and very happy. The seed had somehow been planted some years ago in our counseling sessions and was now bearing fruit. Sometimes, it just takes time.

A final idea that I wanted to share with you about my years as a psychotherapist, Colleen, is that sometimes we might think we are helping someone in one way and later discover that we have been helping them in quite another way. We might not even realize it at the time. A doctor shared his experience of this as a fellow in an emergency room in a large inner city hospital. Many of his patients who were admitted to his care died of drug overdoses. Most of them were young, very close to his own age—people that he deeply cared about. After a few months of this, he became overwhelmed by a sense of futility and became quite depressed.

This doctor happened to be a Buddhist and it had always been his practice to pray for his patients. When a patient died, he would light a candle on his altar at home, pray for each person daily, and keep it burning for a month. Reflecting on this practice many years later, he said that he had begun to wonder that perhaps the reason he was there was not what he had thought. He had expected to serve by trying to cure his patients. When their problems proved resistant to his medical expertise, he had felt useless. But maybe he was not meant to be there to cure people. Perhaps he was there so that no one would die without someone to pray for them. Perhaps he had served every one of his patients more than he would ever know.

As counselors, Colleen, maybe the greatest blessing we offer others is the belief we have in their struggle for freedom; the courage to support and accompany them as they determine for themselves the strength that will become their refuge and the foundation of their lives. I think it is especially important to believe in someone at a time when they cannot yet believe in themselves. Then your belief will become their lifeline. As one young gay man told me, "you have seen me and I am grateful." Everyone wants to be seen and accepted for who they are. As counselors we have an opportunity to do this—to affirm their person. Sometimes, simply being accepted as you are and cared about by another can affect a person in very profound ways.

6

How Love Goes On

IN OUR CULTURE, IT is never easy or uplifting to talk about death and dying. But because it is an important part of our lives, I wanted to offer some reflections about it.

The satirist, Woody Allen, once said, "in America, death is seen as optional."[1] In a culture where few are even willing to grow old, it is not surprising that death is sometimes viewed as if it were a social problem. Once, when a lady who was in the last stages of cancer was asked how she felt about dying, she said that she felt "embarrassed." Another person said that she was afraid that she would not be able to die a good death. When she was asked what she meant by that, she said, "I worry that I will not be able to do things properly," like the anxiety she might feel about a dinner party going badly. Maybe our culture wants us to believe that if death is not preventable, then perhaps it can be made socially acceptable.

I am seventy-five years old now and I must truthfully confess that I think more about dying now than when I was younger. I think that is true for most people as they grow older. In addition, my thoughts and ideas have matured through the years. As I reflect on this topic now, it seems to me that as Christians, we live our lives backwards. What I mean by this, Colleen, is that the way we think about death helps to determine how we think about life. It gives us that "blueprint" for living. Having been raised a Catholic, I was

---

1. Quoted from brainyquote.com/woodyallen.html.

always taught that there was heaven, hell, and purgatory. The goal of life was to attain heaven and avoid hell. Moreover, when I was young, I tended to think of heaven, hell and purgatory as "places." Heaven was the place where we lived in the presence of God and our loved ones, and everyone was always completely happy. There would be no more sorrows there. In the same way, hell was a place where there was constant pain and suffering. Sometimes, I even thought that it was a place of constant fire. In a similar way, I was taught that purgatory was a place that you went to for purification. Because you could only get into heaven if you had no stain of sin on your soul, some people might have to go to purgatory for a while in order to be purified. Then, they would go to heaven forever.

This was the very traditional way I was taught about what happens to you when you die. In this understanding, the body is only the dwelling place for the soul and when you die, your body returns to dust but your soul lives on forever. As I have become older, I must say that I am no longer as sure as I was that heaven, hell and purgatory are "places." As some contemporary spiritual writers suggest today, perhaps "going to heaven" has something to do with our understanding of "time" or a "new and different way of being." The same for "going to hell." And the whole idea of purgatory—or our need for it when we die—is misunderstood or at least doubted. Today, some people believe that our sorrows, suffering and difficulties here on earth are really our purgatory. These are our experiences of purification. In any case, these are some of my current thoughts about what happens to us when we die. However, it has been difficult for me to get away from my traditional upbringing about heaven, hell and purgatory. But I think in a good way, these beliefs that I was raised with, have certainly influenced the way I have tried to live my life. I still believe that heaven is a place of complete peace and happiness where we will live forever with God and all our loved ones. And, like all of us, I certainly don't know exactly what that will be like. The same for what we call hell. What that consists of, we just don't know.

But what I would like you to always remember, Colleen, is that our love outlives us and strengthens others, even after we ourselves are gone. I will always love you, Colleen, and in some way, will always be with you. The author John Powell wrote a short book some years ago entitled *Unconditional Love*. In this book, he tells the story of a young man, Tommy, who was one of Powell's students. Tommy was twenty-four years of age and dying of cancer. At one stage, before his death, Tommy comes to Powell and shares with him that he feels there are worse tragedies in life than dying young. Here is part of their conversation.

"What's it like to be only twenty-four and dying?"

"Well, it could be worse."

"Like what?"

"Well, like being fifty and having no values or ideals, like being fifty and thinking that booze, seducing women, and making money are the real 'biggies' in life. . . . The essential sadness is to go through life without loving. But it would be equally sad to go through life and leave this world without ever telling those you loved that you had loved them."[2]

From the mouth of a dying young man we hear a great truth, Colleen. There are only two potential tragedies in life and dying young is not one of them. What is tragic is to go through life without loving and without expressing love and affection toward those whom we do love.

As long as we can love each other, and remember the feeling of love we had, we can die without ever really going away. All the love we created is still there. All the memories are still there. We live on—in the hearts of everyone we have touched and nurtured while we were here on earth. I think this is because love establishes a relationship that can never be broken. Because of death, the relationship changes, but it is still there. As Morrie told Mitch in his book, *Tuesdays with Morrie*, "death ends a life, not a relationship."[3]

It is also true, Colleen, that in our Catholic faith, we believe in the communion of saints. This means because of our baptism and

2. Powell, *Unconditional Love*, 132–33.

3. Albom, *Tuesdays with Morrie*, 174.

participation in the Eucharist, we are all connected to one another. For me, this has been a consoling thought. And it's important to remember this when we die. We are still connected—still in relationship to one another—only in a different way. But because of this, Colleen, there is one thing that I would ask of you when I die. Please continue to pray for me. Why? Because if there is such a place—an idea of purgatory where we go to be purified before we can enter heaven—then your prayers for me can be a powerful way that this process of purification will be hastened and I will be able to enter heaven more quickly.

In the final analysis, Colleen, I truly believe in the Lord's mercy and that He will forgive me my sins and bring me into eternal life. I believe that Jesus "is" the mercy of God. I am certainly a sinner but God's grace, mercy and forgiveness will be stronger than sin and death. A friend of mine that I thought was a very holy man said that when he died and met St. Peter at the "pearly gates" of heaven, he would only speak one word—"mercy." I think that will also be my word.

I am now in the evening of my life, Colleen, and I would like to join in the words of St. Paul to his friend Timothy. "As for me, my life is already being poured out as a libation, and the time has come for me to be gone. I have fought the good fight to the end; I have run the race to the finish; I have kept the faith; all there is to come now is the crown of righteousness reserved for me, which the Lord, the righteous judge, will give to me on that Day; and not only to me but to all those who have longed for his Appearing" (2 Tim. 4:6–8).

Finally, always remember, Colleen, that "death ends a life, not a relationship." This is the way that our love for each other will always go on.

Bibliography

Albom, Mitch. *Tuesdays with Morrie: An Old Man, A Young Man, and Life's Greatest Lesson.* New York: Doubleday, 1997.

Coles, Robert. *Dorothy Day: A Radical Devotion.* Reading, MA: Perseus, 1987.

Eliot, T.S. *The Complete Poems and Plays, 1909–1950.* New York: Harcourt, Brace, 1935.

Fox, Matthew. *Breakthrough: Meister Eckhart's Creation Spirituality in New Translation.* Garden City, NY: Image, 1980.

Franklin, R.W., editor. *The Poems of Emily Dickinson.* Cambridge, MA: Harvard University Press, 1999.

Gibran, Kahil. *The Prophet.* New York: Knopf, 1967.

Greene, Graham. *The Honorary Consul.* New York: Penguin, 1973.

Hammarskjold, Dag. *Markings.* London: Faber and Faber, 1964.

Jung, Carl. Commentary on Richard Wilhelm's translation and explanation of *The Secret of the Golden Flower.* New York: Harcourt, Brace, Jovanovich, 1962.

Kazantzakis, Nikos. *The Last Temptation of Christ.* New York: Simon and Shuster, 1960.

Kea, Elizabeth. *Amazed by Grace.* Nashville: Thomas Nelson, 2003.

Keating, Thomas. *The Heart of the World.* New York: Crossroads, 2008.

King, Martin Luther, Jr. "Suffering and Faith." In *A Testament of Hope: The Essential Writings and Speeches of Martin Luther King, Jr.,* edited by James Melvin Washington, 41–42. San Francisco: Harper & Row, 1986.

Kushner, Harold. *How Good Do We Have To Be?* Boston: Little, Brown, 1996.

LeShan, Lawrence. *How to Meditate: A Guide to Self-Discovery.* New York: Bantam, 1974.

May, Rollo. *The Courage to Create.* New York: Bantam, 1975.

Moore, Brian. *The Lonely Passion of Judith Hearne.* Boston: Little, Brown, 1955.

Newman, John Henry. *An Essay on the Development of Christian Doctrine.* Middlesex, England: Penguin, 1974.

Nouwen, Henri. *Bread for the Journey.* San Francisco: Harper, 1997.

Remen, Rachel. *My Grandfather's Blessings.* New York: Riverhead, 2000.

Rilke, Rainer Maria. *Letters to a Young Poet.* New York: Norton, 1934.

Ross, Maggie. *The Fire of Your Life: A Solitude Shared.* New York: Paulist Press, 1983.

Saroyan, William. *The Human Comedy.* New York: Harcourt, Brace, 1943.

Satir, Virginia. *The Family Networker.* 13 (January–February), 28–32.

Steinbeck, John. *East of Eden.* New York: Viking, 1952.

Uhlein, Gabriele, and Hildegard, Saint. *Meditations with Hildegard of Bingen.* Sante Fe, NM, 1983.

Wiesel, Elie. *Night.* Translated by Stella Rodway. New York: Avon, 1960.

Williams, Margery. *The Velveteen Rabbit.* New York: Platt and Munk, 1987.

Zuck, Roy. *The Speaker's Quote Book.* Grand Rapids, MI: Kregel, 2009.

www.ingramcontent.com/pod-product-compliance
Lightning Source LLC
Chambersburg PA
CBHW071050090426
42737CB00013B/2311